Seven Clocks

A Tickin'

Towards Christ's Soon Return

Daniel K. Goodwin

Best-selling Author of God's Final Jubilee

Evangelist Dan Goodwin
117 E. 18th St. #165
Owensboro, KY 42303

www.godsfinaljubilee.com
daniel@godsfinaljubilee.com

ISBN: 978-1-60208-436-0

All Scriptures from the 1611 King James Bible

Edited by Laurie Smith

Printed in the USA by
FBC Publications & Printing
Fort Pierce, FL 34982
www.fbcpublications.com

God's Final Jubilee Ministry Partners

Alan Hatfield, TX
Robyn Dalby, MO
Janet Anweiler, CA
Greg Smith, OH
Cynthia Schleicher, MI
Edmond Doone, FL
Robert Howard, TN
Susan Harrison, IN
Thomas Koch, WA
John Mayhew, IL
Rosemary Lutcavage, NC

Dan & Rhonda Forsman, GA
Neil Kaus, MN
Sue & Greg Carnehl, CO
Paul Anderson, FL
Todd Fagerstrom, WI
Harry Fuchigami, HI
Dennis Anderson, MI
Perry Hampton, NC
Pedro Kwik, SG
Joe Lilly, TX
Donald Cary, VA

Debbie Porter, ME
Lucille Benthall, TX
Vic Lunka, NC
Garry Ashburn, VA
Keith Carpenter, NJ
Gordon Bradley, FL
Keith Schmidlin, MI
Donna Bradley, TX
Phyllis Harden, AR
Edward Carlsen Jr., NY
Richard Gieson, FL
Steve Heller, OK

Zbigniew Komisarz, WA
Ronnie McMillan, NC
Latha Vasa, MD
Alana Carpenter, IA
Leroy & Betty Foster, MO
Sue Mathisen, MN
George P. Marshall, PA
J. S. Brown, AZ
Heather Montague, NC
Heidi Brown, NC
Brian Cavins, IN
Susan Hughes, FL

"About the time of the end, a body of men will be raised up who will turn their attention to the Prophecies, and insist upon their literal interpretation, in the midst of much clamor and opposition."

~ Sir Isaac Newton

* CONTENTS *

Part One

Seven Jewels of Prophecy

Part Two

Seven Ticking Clocks

Introduction

The condition of the world today is like the folks on the *Titanic*: eating, drinking, and being merry, unaware that time is running out and their doom is just hours away. Passengers were unaware of the danger on the horizon, as the enemy was hidden beneath the surface of the ocean. When the iceberg was spotted by the crew, it was already too late.

Like those on the *Titanic*, humanity is unaware of the doom that is lurking just ahead. The world thinks it has plenty of time, but once the trumpet has blown and Christ comes for the saints, it will be too late. It is almost midnight, the seven clocks are ticking, and everything is about to change. Are you ready?

The most prophetic movie I have ever seen is *The Lord of the Rings*. In the story, Frodo has just destroyed the ring. It is the end of an age, and he and Sam have climbed onto a rock to await death. As Armageddon looms, Frodo makes a statement to Sam that is so prophetic for us today:

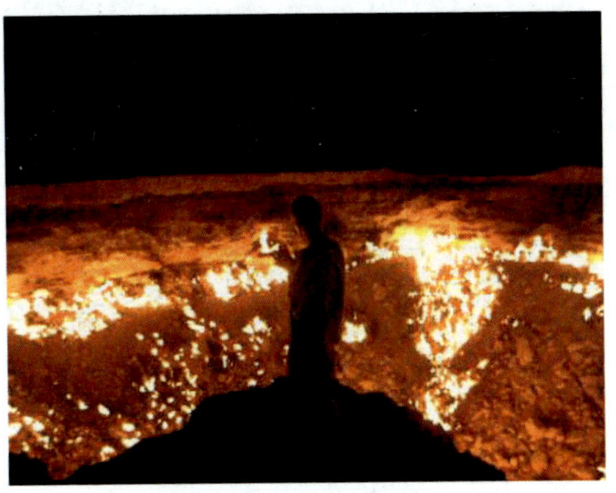

"I'M GLAD TO BE WITH YOU SAMWISE GAMGEE, HERE AT THE END OF ALL THINGS."

Frodo Baggins, *The Lord of the Rings*

Preface

PART ONE: Seven Jewels of Prophecy.

This part explains some basic concepts of prophecy, as likened to the inner components of a clock. A timepiece is made of the mainspring, crown, and hands; however, a wise repairman knows that it is the 'jewels' inside the case that determine both accuracy and dependability of the clock. So too, understanding basic prophetic concepts---or Biblical jewels---will aid us and provide a firm foundation for discerning the accuracy of end-time events.

PART TWO: The Seven Ticking Clocks.

End-time study is the process of revealing God's mysteries, the most exciting of which is the timing of His return and righteous judgement. Thankfully, revelation of the Word points to a perfectly-orchestrated timeline which I've found to be in the form of clocks. Seven of them. All are ticking down and demonstrate His loving promise and purpose for us.

This book is written to help you apply the jewels of prophecy to these ticking clocks. It is my hope that using this book as a guide, you understand the lateness of the hour in which we live and prepare yourself and your loved ones for His return.

<u>If you skip the Seven Jewels in Part One</u> in your excitement to learn about the seven ticking clocks, you will miss some important "jewels" needed to fully "unwind" the startling revelations that I reveal in Part Two. Matthew Henry in the 1800's explains it this way:

"…as Revelation is the last book of the New Testament, and the prophetical books of the Old Testament are placed last… **many (readers, ed.note) run themselves into confusion by beginning their Bible at the wrong end."**

-Matthew Henry, Commentary on the whole Bible

Part One

Seven Jewels of Prophecy

The Biblical jewels that are the foundation of prophecy.

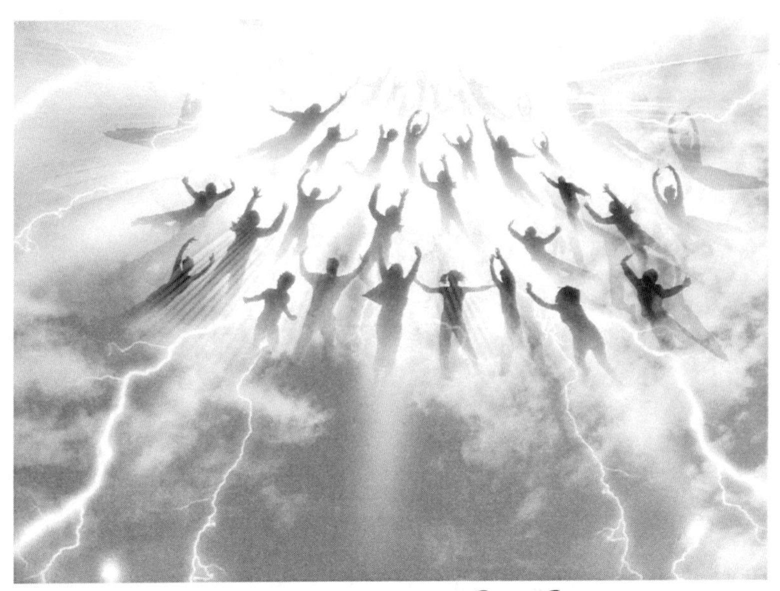

Every person in the last 2000 years who has set a date for the return of the Lord, has been WRONG!

Let that sink in the next time someone tells you they know the date of the rapture.

The Lord intended for us to know the season of His return, not the exact date.

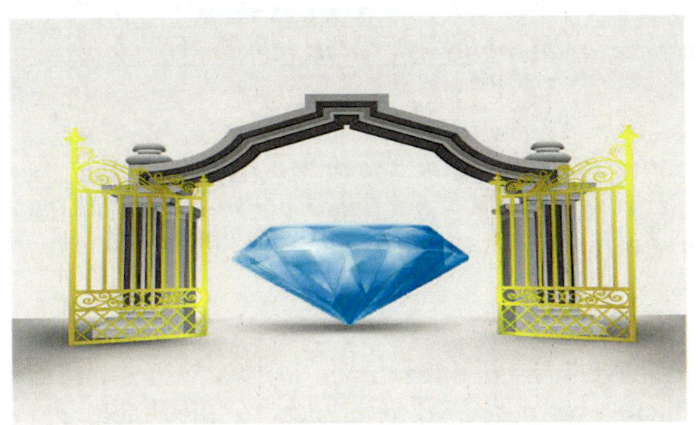

A Rapturous Jewel

Prophecy culminates in the bodily resurrection of the saints that we call the rapture. It is a precious 'jewel' because it is our blessed hope! The word "rapture" is not in the Bible, but words such as trinity and demon, do not appear either, yet they describe important doctrines of our faith. Knowing the origin of the word "rapture" will help to open your understanding of the word. Let me explain.

Rapture Defined

Rapture is derived from the Latin word *rapturo*. The Greek word in the New Testament is *harpazo*, and the English uses the two words *'caught up'*.

Rapturo literally means *"to be taken out of the way, to be gathered, or caught away."* '*Harpazo*' and '*caught up*' also mean the same. Another term is '*translated*' which is used three times in Scripture with the same meaning:

Translated Defined

TRANSLA'TED, *participle passive* Conveyed from one place to another; removed to heaven without dying; rendered into another language.

Colossians 1:13 *"Who hath delivered us from the power of darkness, and hath translated us into the kingdom of his dear Son:"*

Hebrews 11:5 *"By faith Enoch was translated that he should not see death; and was not found, because God had translated him: for before his translation he had this testimony, that he pleased God."*

Translated is used three times in two verses and it is the Biblical word used in reference to the 'rapture'. Since 'rapture' is the word we are most familiar with today; it is the word I use instead of translated.

Caught Up

Acts 8:39 *"And when they were come up out of the water, the Spirit of the Lord caught away Philip, that the eunuch saw him no more: and he went on his way rejoicing."*

The phrase "caught away" is the same as caught up. Philip was caught away by the Spirit to preach elsewhere. Here, it is obviously not talking about the removal of a person to Heaven.

Revelation 12:5 *"And she brought forth a man child, who was to rule all nations with a rod of iron: and her child was caught up unto God, and to his throne."*

The "caught up" in this passage is certainly a rapture, but it is referring to Christ ascending bodily into Heaven.

2 Corinthians 12:2 *"I knew a man in Christ above fourteen years ago, (whether in the body, I cannot tell; or whether out of the body, I cannot tell: God knoweth;) such an one caught up to the third heaven."*

2 Corinthians 12:4 *"How that he was caught up into paradise, and heard unspeakable words, which it is not lawful for a man to utter."*

1Thessalonians 4:17 *"Then we which are alive and remain shall be caught up together with them in the clouds, to meet the Lord in the air: and so shall we ever be with the Lord."*

All these Scriptures where "caught up" is used fit the definition of being gathered or taken away; but only one --- 1 Thessalonians 4:17--- speaks of the rapture of the saints.

More verses referring to the rapture

I Corinthians 15:51-52 "[51]*Behold, I shew you a mystery; We shall not all sleep, but we shall all be changed,* [52]*In a moment, in the twinkling of an eye, at the last trump: for the trumpet shall sound, and the dead shall be raised incorruptible, and we shall be changed."*

Revelation 4:1 *"After this I looked, and, behold, a door was opened in heaven: and the first voice which I heard was as it were of a trumpet talking with me; which said, Come up hither, and I will shew thee things which must be hereafter."*

Pre-, Mid- or Post-Tribulation Rapture?

There are three views concerning *when* the rapture will occur. Pre-Tribulation: the rapture occurs before the Tribulation; mid-Tribulation: the rapture occurs at the middle of the seven-year Tribulation; and post-Tribulation: the rapture occurs at the end.

Rather than take the time to debate the position of the latter two, I will simply tell you why I adhere strongly to a pre-Tribulation view of the rapture.

Proofs of the pre-Tribulation rapture

1.The rapture is imminent. In other words, the rapture

could happen any moment! God has not told us the specific day or hour of His return. If the rapture were to happen at the middle or the end of the Tribulation, it would be easy to pinpoint it to the very day based on the events laid out in the opening of the seals in the book of Revelation.

2. The rapture is our "blessed hope."
Titus 2:13 *"Looking for that blessed hope, and the glorious appearing of the great God and our Saviour Jesus Christ;"*

The "blessed hope" of the rapture is that Christ comes and delivers us from the wrath to come upon the world. It would not be considered the blessed hope at the middle or at the end of the Tribulation. Praise the Lord! He will "catch His bride away" BEFORE the wrath starts!

3. The Lord has not appointed us to wrath. The Tribulation is the wrath of God upon this world as well as God dealing with Israel. Revelation makes it plain that the entire Tribulation is God's wrath, not just the second half.

Revelation 6:16 *"And said to the mountains and rocks, Fall on us, and hide us from the face of him that sitteth on the throne, and from the wrath of the Lamb:"*

God has not appointed the saints to wrath. Do not confuse chastisement and persecution believers go through with God's wrath; they are two separate things entirely.

1 Thessalonians 5:9 *"For God hath not appointed us to wrath, but to obtain salvation by our Lord Jesus Christ,"*

Romans 8:1 *"There is therefore now no condemnation to them which are in Christ Jesus, who walk not after the flesh, but after the Spirit."*

John 5:24 *"Verily, verily, I say unto you, He that heareth my word, and believeth on him that sent me, hath everlasting life, and shall not come into condemnation; but is passed from death unto life."*

Revelation 3:10 *"Because thou hast kept the word of my patience, I also will keep thee from the hour of temptation, which shall come upon all the world, to try them that dwell upon the earth."*

In addition, Daniel 9:24-27 teaches the Tribulation is the seventieth week of years for Israel and has nothing to do with the church.

4. There is no mention of the church after Revelation 4:1. The seven churches are mentioned in Revelation 2 and 3. The rapture takes place in chapter 4:1 followed by the opening of the seals during the Tribulation. The reason the church is not mentioned again until the end of Revelation is that all believers have been taken out at the rapture. The true church will be gone; God will once again deal with the Jews in the 70th week mentioned in Daniel 9:27, which is the final week (seven years) of the Old Testament. (The entire Church Age was grafted in between Daniel's 69th and 70th week.

* We will look more at Daniel 9 in another chapter.

5. The Restrainer---the Holy Spirit of God who indwells all believers---has been removed. It is believed that the Antichrist comes on the scene as the first horseman at the **beginning** of the seven-year Tribulation as indicated in the following verses.

Revelation 6:1-2 *"[1]And I saw when the Lamb opened one of the seals, and I heard, as it were the noise of thunder, one of the four beasts saying, Come and see. [2]And I saw, and behold a white horse: and he that sat on him had a bow; and a crown was given unto him: and he went forth conquering, and to conquer."*

This white horse carries the Antichrist into the position of One World dictator at the opening of the first of the seven seals. This scene is at the beginning of the seven-year Tribulation.

Do not confuse the Antichrist with Jesus who comes on a white horse in Revelation 19:11 at the end of the Tribulation. Satan is the great counterfeiter. He has a counterfeit of everything God has. He has counterfeit Bibles, counterfeit churches, and a counterfeit spirit. Here we see that the Antichrist is the counterfeit Messiah. He comes on a white horse just as Jesus will seven years later.

I want to show you that this Antichrist, this man of sin, does not show up until *after* the Restrainer, that indwells all believers, is taken away. It is vital that you see this! Paul makes this perfectly clear in this passage.

2 Thessalonians 2:1-8 *"1Now we beseech you, brethren, by the coming of our Lord Jesus Christ, and by our gathering together unto him, 2That ye be not soon shaken in mind, or be troubled, neither by spirit, nor by word, nor by letter as from us, as that the day of Christ is at hand. 3Let no man deceive you by any means: for that day shall not come, except there come a falling away first, and that man of sin be revealed, the son of perdition; 4Who opposeth and exalteth himself above all that is called God, or that is worshipped; so that he as God sitteth in the temple of God, shewing himself that he is God. 5Remember ye not, that, when I was yet with you, I told you these things? 6And now ye know what withholdeth that he might be revealed in his time. 7For the mystery of iniquity doth already work: only he who now letteth will let, until he be taken out of the way. 8And then shall that Wicked be revealed, whom the Lord shall consume with the spirit of his mouth, and shall destroy with the brightness of his coming:"*

Notice in verse 2, "*the day of Christ*" is the second coming of Christ at the end of the seven-year Tribulation. When you look at the context of the passage back in 2 Thessalonians 1:7-12, it is obvious that the "day of Christ" in 2 Thessalonians 2:2 is speaking of the second coming at the end of the Tribulation.

2 Thessalonians 1:7-12 *"[7]And to you who are troubled rest with us, when the Lord Jesus shall be revealed from heaven with his mighty angels, [8]In flaming fire taking vengeance on them that know not God, and that obey not the gospel of our Lord Jesus Christ: [9]Who shall be punished with everlasting destruction from the presence of the Lord, and from the glory of his power; [10]When he shall come to be glorified in his saints, and to be admired in all them that believe (because our testimony among you was believed) in that day. [11]Wherefore also we pray always for you, that our God would count you worthy of this calling, and fulfil all the good pleasure of his goodness, and the work of faith with power: [12]That the name of our Lord Jesus Christ may be glorified in you, and ye in him, according to the grace of our God and the Lord Jesus Christ."*

With a clear teaching that the Antichrist arrives at the first seal in Revelation 6, which is at the beginning of the Tribulation, let us go back to 2 Thessalonians 2:1-8 and see proof that <u>no believers will be here when the first seal is opened.</u> This passage clearly teaches that, again, the Holy Spirit, which is the 'restrainer' that indwells all believers, will be removed before the Antichrist comes on the scene.

2 Thessalonians 2:6-8 *"[6]And now ye know what withholdeth that he might be revealed in his time. <u>[7]For the mystery of iniquity doth already work: only he who now letteth will let, until he be taken out of the way. [8]And then shall that Wicked be revealed,</u> whom the Lord shall consume with the spirit of his mouth, and shall destroy with the brightness of his*

coming:"
The "*what withholdth*" is the Holy Spirit of God who indwells all believers. He restrains (letteth) the work of Satan until he is *"taken out of the way"* at the rapture. Therefore, there cannot be any doubt that the rapture is *before* the Tribulation.

The Holy Spirit cannot leave without us, my friend! He indwells all believers. This passage teaches that all believers, along with the Holy Spirit's influence and restraining power, will be removed *right before the Antichrist is revealed.* All the "salt and light" will be gone. That is the rapture folks!

6. Old Testament types of the rapture.

a. Enoch was removed from God's wrath *before* the floods came.
b. Lot was delivered from Sodom *before* the fire fell.
c. Noah was lifted up above the waters *while* the floods came.

7. The contrast between the rapture and the second coming.
These two events simply *cannot* be at the same time or be the same event. The Scriptures clearly convey this; here are a few that illustrate the point:

Rapture	**Second Coming**
Coming for us John 14:4, 1 Thess. 4:14-17	Coming with us Rev. 19:14, Jude 1:14
As a thief in the night 1 Thess. 5:2	Every eye shall see Him Rev. 1:7
Meets us in the clouds 1 Thess. 4:16-17	Coming on a white horse Rev. 19:11
Imminent 1 Thess. 5:4-6, Luke 12:40	At end of seven years 2 Thess. 2:3-8

8. The testimony of men of old. The rapture is not a new teaching, as is claimed by some. It has been taught for centuries. Here are some quotes from time past:

"I will add this more, namely, what may be conceived to be the cause of this **RAPTURE** of the saints on high to meet the Lord in the clouds, rather than to wait his coming to earth....What if it be, that they may be PRESERVED during the Conflagration of the earth and the works thereof, 2 Peter 3:10, that as Noah and his family were preserved from the Deluge by being lift up above the waters in the Ark; so should the saints at the Conflagration be lift up in the clouds unto their Ark, Christ, to be preserved there from the deluge of fire, wherein the wicked shall be consumed?" ("The Works of Joseph Mede," 1672, London edition, Book IV, p.776)

"**And therefore, when in the end the Church shall be suddenly caught up from this**, it is said, "There shall be tribulation such as has not been since the beginning, neither shall be." For this is the last contest of the righteous, in which, when they overcome they are crowned with incorruption." Irenaeus in his book "Against Heresies" 130-202 A.D. He was an eyewitness to the apostle John and a disciple of Polycarp.

"We who see that terrible things have begun, and know that still more terrible things are imminent, may regard it as the greatest advantage to depart from it as quickly as possible. Do you not give God thanks, do you not congratulate yourself, **that by an early departure you are taken away, and delivered from the shipwrecks and disasters that are imminent?**"
From the "Treatise of Cyprian" (200 AD – 258 AD)

"For all the saints and elect of God are gathered, prior to the tribulation that is to come, and are taken to the Lord lest they see the confusion that is to overwhelm the world because of our sins.
Ephraim the Syrian in his work, "*On The Last Times 2*" (306 AD – 373 AD)

The Rapture was a mystery revealed to Apostle Paul

The Bible is a book of mysteries, of that I am more convinced each day. A mystery is something that was always there, but not understood.

Webster's 1828 dictionary defines "mystery" as follows:

MYS'TERY 1. A profound secret; something wholly unknown or something kept cautiously concealed, and therefore exciting curiosity or wonder; such as the *mystery* of the man with the iron mask in France.

The rapture is just such a mystery, but nobody understood until it was revealed by the Apostle Paul. There can be no doubt that the Old Testament people did not know of the rapture. Look at the following Scripture:

1 Corinthians 15:50-52 *"[50]Now this I say, brethren, that flesh and blood cannot inherit the kingdom of God; neither doth corruption inherit incorruption. [51]Behold, I shew you a mystery; We shall not all sleep, but we shall all be changed, [52]In a moment, in the twinkling of an eye, at the last trump: for the trumpet shall sound, and the dead shall be raised incorruptible, and we shall be changed."*

The rapture has shadows and figures in the Old Testament, such as Enoch and Lot, but nobody before Paul would have seen the rapture as a type in any of these Old Testament stories. You and I can look back and see these types because the mystery of the rapture has been revealed. Everyone before the time of Paul was ignorant of the rapture until God enlightened the Apostle Paul about it. The prophet Daniel was told "*...seal the book, even to the time of the end...*" (Daniel 12:4). In other words, God was going to keep some things a mystery until a later generation came on the scene. We are that generation.

The most misused phrase in all of Christianity!

I am going to expose the unscriptural use of the concept, **"No man knows the day or hour of the rapture."** What do the Scriptures *really* say; and what are they referring to? In the following discourse, I am going to uncover the truth of this hidden mystery.

1. The rapture was revealed to Paul after Acts 9.
2. The mystery was revealed to Paul here: 1 Corinthians 15:51-52 "[51]*Behold, I shew you a*

mystery; We shall not all sleep, but we shall all be changed, [52]In a moment, in the twinkling of an eye, at the last trump: for the trumpet shall sound, and the dead shall be raised incorruptible, and we shall be changed."

3. Remember, a mystery is something that was always there but was hidden from view. The rapture was not understood, nor was it spoken of in Scripture until the ministry of Paul began.

4. There are figures and types of the rapture in the Old Testament, such as Lot and Enoch, but the doctrine itself was not understood. The Old Testament saints were looking for the Kingdom, not the rapture.

5. Therefore, one must conclude that many of the verses people are using to teach that no man knows the day, or the hour are, in fact, taken out of context.

6. Many of those passages quoted are, upon further study, speaking of the *second* coming of Christ to set up the Kingdom.

7. The rapture was not spoken of by Jesus or the apostles in the four Gospels! This means that the rapture is NOT being referred to in Matthew 24. The gleanings* at the end of the Tribulation are certainly spoken of in Matthew 24, but not the pre-Tribulation rapture. Much of Matthew 24 and Mark 13 are speaking of events during the Tribulation.

   * "Gleanings" is the resurrection of the saints alive at the end of the Tribulation.

8. There are no Scriptures before Acts 9 that speak about the rapture.

In conclusion, Scriptures often used to teach 'no man knows the day or hour of the rapture' are speaking about the second coming of Christ to set up the Kingdom. Since we cannot know the day nor the hour of His second coming, neither can we know the day or hour of His coming in the clouds at the rapture. Here are some of the commonly used verses that have been used out of context:

Matthew 24:36 *"But of that day and hour knoweth no man, no, not the angels of heaven, but my Father only."*

Matthew 24:42 *"Watch therefore: for ye know not what hour your Lord doth come."*

Matthew 25:13 *"Watch therefore, for ye know neither the day nor the hour wherein the Son of man cometh."*

Mark 13:32 *"But of that day and that hour knoweth no man, no, not the angels which are in heaven, neither the Son, but the Father."*

Mark 13:33 *"Take ye heed, watch and pray: for ye know not when the time is."*

Mark 13:35 *"Watch ye therefore: for ye know not when the master of the house cometh, at even, or at midnight, or at the cockcrowing, or in the morning:"*

Acts 1:7 *"And he said unto them, It is not for you to know the times or the seasons, which the Father hath put in his own power."*

Remember…
The rapture was a mystery revealed to Paul, by the Spirit, AFTER Acts 9. It was not spoken of in the Gospels at all!

Wedding Jewels

When a man proposes to a woman, he offers her a costly jewel. In many cultures, it is a diamond ring. It is a token of her high value to the man and becomes a treasured heirloom for both man and wife as the years of marriage progress. So too, we are offered jewels of prophetic significance in the wedding customs practiced in Biblical times. Many of these truths are missed simply because of our ignorance of these traditions. By understanding them, a whole new foundation can be built for prophetic truth. These 'jewels' have been a mystery to most of God's people, but they don't have to be anymore.

Jewish Wedding Customs: Type of Christ and His Church

Revelation 21:9 *"... Come hither, **I will shew thee the bride, the Lamb's wife."***

The customs that revolve around the Jewish wedding are based upon Biblical truths concerning Christ coming to claim His bride. The pre-Tribulation rapture will unfold before your very eyes as we look at the beautiful and prophetic Jewish customs of how a young man chose his bride. In Revelation 21:9, we see that all believers are one day going to be the bride of Christ. One day soon when He comes for us at the rapture, for the first time ever, all believers will be a church assembled together in perfect unity without spot or blemish.

The following is a step-by-step process of how a Jewish man obtained his bride in Bible days according to Jewish customs. I want you to see how it coincides with Bible prophecy so that the truth can reinforce your beliefs concerning the things that are shortly to come to pass!

1. The man would make his offer to purchase his bride. We see this in the story of Rebekah in Genesis 24. This offer would be with the permission of the girl's father of course. There may or may not have been some courting, the man could even be a stranger to her, as in the case of Isaac and Rebekah. The woman could only be his bride if she consented willingly, and the groom paid a price for her. Likewise, you and I also were purchased at a great price: Acts 20:28 *"...the church of God, which he hath purchased with his own blood."* However, He does not force us to be His bride; we must choose to accept Him and His payment. Some similarities of Rebekah and a person trusting Christ:

- **a.** Rebekah trusted a person she had never seen, just as you and I must trust a Saviour we have only heard about through the Scriptures.
- **b.** She received a free gift. Our salvation is a free gift from God. Romans 6:23 "*... but the gift of God is eternal life through Jesus Christ our Lord."*
- **c.** She left her kingdom for his kingdom. One day you and I will leave earth and enter His Kingdom.
- **d.** It was an act of her free will. "Whosoever will..."

2. A marriage contract would be given. This contract spells out the conditions, inheritance, and obligations of the marriage (Jacob had a contract for both of his wives). This would be like the vows that a husband makes at the altar. Just as the groom gives the bride a contract, so too, Jesus has given us His word, the Bible, as a covenant filled with His promises to us.

John 14:1-3 *"[1]Let not your heart be troubled: ye believe in God, believe also in me. [2]In my Father's house are many mansions: if it were not so, I would have told you. I go to prepare a place for you. [3]And if I go and prepare a place for you, I will come again, and receive you unto myself; that where I am, there ye may be also."*

3. When the bride accepted and received the purchase price, she became formally betrothed or espoused. The actual ceremony may not take place for months, and there is no physical contact until the ceremony (Story of Joseph and Mary). Betrothed means contracted for future marriage. Espoused means promised in marriage by contract. She will continue to live with her parents until he returns for her. Likewise, when you and I accept the free gift of eternal life, we are saved and become the purchased property of Christ immediately, but we have no physical contact until our wedding day. We are espoused to Christ but are not actually the bride until He comes for us at the rapture.

2 Corinthians 11:22 *"For I am jealous over you with godly jealousy: for I have espoused you to one husband, that I may present you as a chaste virgin to Christ."*

4. The groom would go back to his father's house to prepare the bridal chamber for his bride.

- **a.** He leaves the purchase price with her, as a guarantee. Likewise, we receive the Holy Spirit as a down payment, a surety that He is coming for us.

Ephesians 1:14 *"Which is the earnest of our inheritance until the redemption of the purchased possession, unto the praise of his glory."*

You cannot get any more eternally secure than that!

- **b.** The groom may be gone for a long time. Our Saviour has been gone for nearly 2,000 years now!
- **c.** He promised to return for her. The bride is to watch and wait.

John 14:2b-3 *"... I go to prepare a place for you. And if I go and prepare a place for you, I will come again, and receive you unto myself; that where I am, there ye may be also."*

Jesus has gone back to the Father's house. He is preparing a place for His bride. As soon as it is ready, He is coming back for us! That will be the rapture, the *end* of the Church Age.

5. The espoused bride is to prepare herself for his return.

- **a.** It is in her marriage contract to do so. Our marriage contract is the Bible. We are to be growing in grace and preparing for His return.
- **b.** She was to purify herself and keep herself for only him.
  2 Corinthians 11:2 *"For I am jealous over you with godly jealousy: for I have espoused you to one husband, that I may present you as a chaste virgin to Christ."*
- **c.** She was to be ready and waiting to go with him at any moment! She was to have her bags packed and be ready to go. We also, are to be ready at any moment for the coming of Christ. This is just another proof that the rapture is *before* the Tribulation, and that it could happen at any moment.

Revelation 19:7 *"Let us be glad and rejoice, and give honour to him: for the marriage of the Lamb is come, and his wife hath made herself ready."*

6. Only the father of the groom would know the date of the wedding. Neither the bride nor the groom knows the date. It is the *father* who decides when the house is ready.

Matthew 24:36 *"But of that day and hour knoweth no man, no, not the angels of heaven, but my Father only."*

7. The espoused bride lights an oil lamp for the groom each night. She is expecting and hoping he will come that night. It would help the groom find her window at night, as well as let other men know she is espoused. Hey, does the world's crowd know that you belong to the King of Kings? Oil is also symbolic of the Holy Ghost. The light symbolizes Jesus, the light of the world. Now you will better understand the parable of the ten virgins in Matthew 25 next time you read it. Five had oil and five did not. If oil is a symbol of the Holy Spirit, then five of those virgins were lost.

8. When the father decided that it was time, he would send his son to get his bride and would prepare for the ceremony.

- **a.** This announcement was made to the son with the sounding of trumpets. 1 Corinthians 15:51-57, 1 Thessalonians 4:16 and Revelation 4:1, all speak of the rapture occurring with a trumpet.
- **b.** Guests are invited to the wedding.
- **c.** A shout was made at the door. This was the signal for the bride to rush out to meet him, as well as for modesty's sake. The groom would meet her at the door and carry her out. (This may be where we got the tradition of carrying the bride over the threshold). Hey, at the rapture *we* will be "caught up!" It is very possible, considering this, that the trumpet is heard only in Heaven.
- **d.** The neighbors will not even know you left.

9. The wedding ceremony takes place. At the wedding would be the Rabbi, the best man, two witnesses, family and friends.

10. The couple would enter the bridal chamber and have a seven-day honeymoon. This symbolizes the seven years we are in Heaven while the Tribulation takes place on the earth. While we are eating cake in Heaven, the terrible Tribulation is taking place down on earth. What a contrast! Where will you be?

Also, this is when the type of the Judgement Seat will take place. This doesn't refer to when *sin* is judged, that took place at Cavalry for all Saints when Jesus took the punishment for our sins. It refers to when the groom will brag on the good qualities of his bride. So, the Judgment Seat is where our *works* are judged.

1 Corinthians 3:13-15 *"[13]Every man's work shall be made manifest: for the day shall declare it, because it shall be revealed by fire; and the fire shall try every man's work of what sort it is. [14]If any man's work abide which he hath built thereupon, he shall receive a reward. [15]If any man's work shall be burned, he shall suffer loss: but he himself shall be saved; yet so as by fire."*

This is the time that crowns are awarded for our works. How sad that some will be left with nothing but ashes.

Jesus began His ministry with a wedding (John 2), and He will end His ministry with a wedding after He raptures us away into heaven.

Discerning Jewels

The watch repairman has to be knowledgeable to properly diagnose and service a timepiece. He will be sure to inspect, examine, and discern the condition of the jewels and inner workings so that accurate and dependable time is ensured. Even so, the watchman on the wall must know how to rightly divide, to discern, and to have keen understanding of the Word and its proper interpretation if he is to comprehend prophetic events. When we study and follow Old Testament stories, and Jesus' parables and teachings, a simple pattern of "discerning jewels" is revealed. I teach them as the three ways to interpret Scripture.

Literal-Figurative-Prophetic

Nothing has helped my study of the Bible quite as much as an understanding of these three ways to look at the Scripture. Often you hear of men who argue and fight over the interpretation of a passage of Scripture. The funny thing is, sometimes both men are right, but both are wrong at the same time! In other words, one guy states the literal interpretation while the other is looking at it figuratively. Both may be exactly right in what they are saying.

If you grasp this, it will forever change the way you study the Bible. The truth is, many of you are already looking at passages in the Bible in the way I am going to describe, but don't realize it. If I can get you to understand the three ways to look at Scripture, you will be shocked how the Bible will open to you like never before.

This is not a strange doctrine; it is the way Jesus looked at Scripture, as well as Peter, Paul and most preachers you've ever listened to.

Three different views of Scripture can ALL be true? Absolutely! For example, one view says the days in Genesis 1 are literal 24-hour days. For the record, I agree 100 percent with that belief. However, another view teaches that those days are prophetic of 1,000-year periods of history. I want to go on record today that I believe that to be 100 percent true as well! Now, can both views be correct? Of course, they can. The first view is the *literal* interpretation. The second view is the *prophetic* interpretation. Both views are different, but both are the truth.

The prophetic view is often the hardest to see. I have been studying prophecy for many years, so things seem to jump out at me more easily than for others. I am not saying that in every verse or passage you read you will find a figurative or a prophetic truth. I am saying that we ought to be always *looking* for it.

Jesus interpreted Scriptures in this manner:

John 3:14 *"And as Moses lifted up the serpent in the wilderness, even so must the Son of man be lifted up:"*

John 6:49 *"Your fathers did eat manna in the wilderness, and are dead."*

Matthew 12:40 *"For as Jonas was three days and three nights in the whale's belly; so shall the Son of man be three days and three nights in the heart of the earth."*

In all these passages, the Lord took a literal Bible story and used it figuratively to teach a truth. The apostle Peter used the creative week in Genesis 1 and interpreted it prophetically.

2 Peter 3:3-8 *"[3]Knowing this first, that there shall come in the last days scoffers, walking after their own lusts, [4]And saying, Where is the promise of his coming? for since the fathers fell asleep, all things continue as they were from the beginning of the creation. [5]For this they willingly are ignorant of, that by the word of God the heavens were of old, and the earth standing out of the water and in the water: [6]Whereby the world that then was, being overflowed with water, perished: [7]But the heavens and the earth, which are now, by the same word are kept in store, reserved unto fire against the day of judgment and perdition of ungodly men. [8]But, beloved, be not ignorant of this one thing, that one day is with the Lord as a thousand years, and a thousand years as one day."*

The Apostle Paul used the Old Testament figuratively

Galatians 4:22-28 *"[22]For it is written, that Abraham had two sons, the one by a bondmaid, the other by a freewoman. [23]But he who was of the bondwoman was born after the flesh; but he of the freewoman was by promise. [24]Which things are an allegory: for these are the two covenants; the one from the mount Sinai, which gendereth to bondage, which is Agar. [25]For this Agar is mount Sinai in Arabia, and answereth to Jerusalem which now is, and is in bondage with her children. [26]But Jerusalem which is above is free, which is the mother of us all. [27]For it is written, Rejoice, thou barren that bearest not; break forth and cry, thou that travailest not: for the desolate hath many more children than she which hath an husband. [28]Now we, brethren, as Isaac was, are the children of promise."*

Paul obviously looked at Scriptures of the Old Testament in a figurative and sometimes prophetic way. **It is right and wise that you and I should do the same.** I could go on and give example after example, but I think I have made my point. I would venture to guess that 95 percent of the folks reading this book have heard a sermon about being a lukewarm Christian at least once and probably more than once in their life.

Revelation 3:15 "I know thy works, that thou art neither cold nor hot: I would thou wert cold or hot."

I have preached this more than once myself. Regardless of where you heard it, the message is no doubt the same. We should strive in our walk with God not to become a "lukewarm" Christian. The interesting thing about it is that the passage used in Revelation 3 is not speaking about an individual believer at all. The passage is speaking about a church becoming lukewarm. That is the literal interpretation. However, it is perfectly right to use the passage figuratively and prophetically when appropriate. After all, the whole Bible is filled with figurative lessons for us.

There are many figures and types in the Bible that have a prophetic interpretation. Since we were just looking at the lukewarm church in Revelation, let's go ahead and use the seven churches listed in Revelation 2 and 3 for our first example.

The Seven Churches

<u>1. Literal interpretation.</u> There were seven, literal churches that existed in that day. They give us insight into Christ's ownership and relationship to the church. They also show us the relationship between the pastor of the church and the Lord. These churches show us what a church ought to be, as well as some things a church ought not to be. This is a simple literal interpretation. These seven churches all existed in 96 A.D. when John got the Revelation from the Lord while on the Isle of Patmos.

2. Figurative interpretation. Truths concerning these seven churches can also be applied to the Christian life. For instance, the church in Ephesus had left its first love. You and I ought to examine our own lives. Do we have a love for Christ and a love for souls that we once had? Take some time to consider the good and bad about each church and see how you measure up. See, this is looking at the seven churches figuratively.

3. Prophetic interpretation. Though I believe these literal churches existed in John's day, **I believe the main prophetic teaching concerning these churches is that they are the seven ages of church history** which will be discussed in Part Two.

Mary and Martha

Did you ever consider the prophetic lessons concerning Mary, Martha, and Lazarus? As you know, Mary and Martha were sisters, and Lazarus was their brother. There are several passages in the Bible where they are mentioned interacting with the Lord. There are some obvious and interesting types and prophetic lessons we can learn from them. For instance, look at the passage where Martha is busy in the kitchen and Mary is sitting at the feet of Jesus.

Luke 10:38-42 *"38Now it came to pass, as they went, that he entered into a certain village: and a certain woman named Martha received him into her house. 39And she had a sister called Mary, which also sat at Jesus' feet, and heard his word. 40But Martha was cumbered about much serving, and came to him, and said, Lord, dost thou not care that my sister hath left me to serve alone? bid her therefore that she help me. 41And Jesus answered and said unto her, Martha, Martha, thou art careful and troubled about many things: 42But one thing is needful: and Mary hath chosen that good part, which shall not be taken away from her."*

This is a literal event that happened during the life of Christ, but there is a figurative lesson taught here too. The lesson is about servitude and worship. We need to be about both, but it is plain which is most important. Then we have this passage about Mary, Martha, and Lazarus:

John 11:1-8 "*[1]Now a certain man was sick, named Lazarus, of Bethany, the town of Mary and her sister Martha. [2](It was that Mary which anointed the Lord with ointment, and wiped his feet with her hair, whose brother Lazarus was sick.) [3]Therefore his sisters sent unto him, saying, Lord, behold, he whom thou lovest is sick. [4]When Jesus heard that, he said, This sickness is not unto death, but for the glory of God, that the Son of God might be glorified thereby. [5]Now Jesus loved Martha, and her sister, and Lazarus. [6]When he had heard therefore that he was sick, he abode two days still in the same place where he was. [7]Then after that saith he to his disciples, Let us go into Judaea again. [8]His disciples say unto him, Master, the Jews of late sought to stone thee; and goest thou thither again?*"

This is also a literal event that happened during the life of Christ. The story goes all the way through verse 45 if you want to read it all. It is even mentioned in several other Scriptures. There are not only figurative lessons here, but a tremendous prophetic interpretation as well.

Consider this…

Lazarus represents "*the dead in Christ shall rise first.*" Wow!

Martha is a type of the Gentile/Church Age saints. When Jesus arrived, she went out *first* to meet the Lord. There is the rapture.

Mary: She represents the Jews. She comes out later, after Martha is gone. Once the rapture takes place and the Church Age saints are removed from the earth, God will once again turn His attention to the Jews! God is not done with them!

Interesting is it not?
We see in these verses that Christ has a deep love for the Jews.

John 11:33-35 *"[33]When Jesus therefore saw her weeping, and the Jews also weeping which came with her, he groaned in the spirit, and was troubled, [34]And said, Where have ye laid him? They said unto him, Lord, come and see. [35]Jesus wept."*

Figures, types, and shadows explained

God's Word best defines these concepts:

Colossians 2:16-17 *"[16]Let no man therefore judge you in meat, or in drink, or in respect of an holyday, or of the new moon, or of the sabbath days: [17]Which are a shadow of things to come; but the body is of Christ."*

1 Corinthians 10:1-4 *"[1]Moreover, brethren, I would not that ye should be ignorant, how that all our fathers were under the cloud, and all passed through the sea; [2]And were all baptized unto Moses in the cloud and in the sea; [3]And did all eat the same spiritual meat; [4]And did all drink the same spiritual drink: for they drank of that spiritual Rock that followed them: and that Rock was Christ."*

Hebrews 8:5 *"Who serve unto the example and shadow of heavenly things, as Moses was admonished of God when he was about to make the tabernacle: for, See, saith he, that thou make all things according to the pattern shewed to thee in the mount."*

Hebrews 9:24 *"For Christ is not entered into the holy places made with hands, which are the figures of the true; but into heaven itself, now to appear in the presence of God for us:"*

Hebrews 10:1 *"For the law having a shadow of good things to come, and not the very image of the things, can never with those sacrifices which they offered year by year continually make the comers thereunto perfect."*

Hebrews 11:19 *"Accounting that God was able to raise him up, even from the dead; from whence also he* *<u>received him in a figure."</u>*

A shadow is a cloudy replica of the real thing.

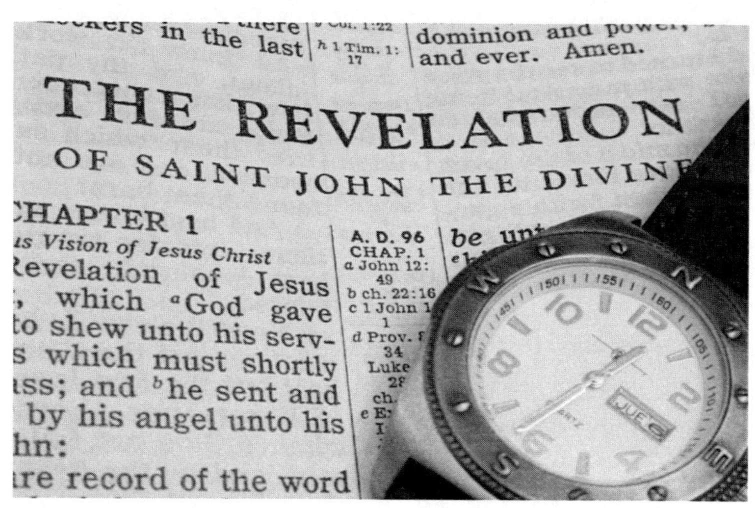

Revelation Jewels

Everyone is fascinated by the book of Revelation, but very few comprehend the message it proclaims. I want to help unveil the 'jewels' hidden in the pages of this final book in the Bible. There are so many great gems just waiting to be discovered by those who are willing to dig for them. I will give a summary of the entire book which is especially pertinent for us today.

"Doubtless much which is designedly obscure to us will be clear to those for whom it was written as the time approaches."

-C. I. Scofield

This is a quote from the introduction to the Revelation in the famous 1906 Scofield Reference Bible. Reverend Scofield is saying there are things in the Bible that will not be fully understood until the generation for which they were written. Let that profound thought sink in! I believe that time is *now*, everything is about to change; the clock is ticking down!

A Passion for Jewels

God promises a special blessing to those who read, hear, and keep the things written in Revelation.

Revelation 1:3 "*Blessed is he that readeth, and they that hear the words of this prophecy, and keep those things which are written therein: for the time is at hand.*"

Readeth means just that, read the book of Revelation. ***Hear*** means to read with a desire to understand it. ***Keep*** means to put into practice the things it says. The blessing is not to the casual reader, but to the one who has a desire and a passion to learn and apply the truth of the Word of God. This is a Bible principle concerning Revelation that will help you with any book of the Bible. Decide you are going to READ the Bible with purpose, seriousness, and a commitment to OBEY what you learn.

Psalm 39:3 "*My heart was hot within me, while I was musing the fire burned: then spake I with my tongue…*"

Joshua 1:8 "*This book of the law shall not depart out of thy mouth; but thou shalt meditate therein day and night, that thou mayest observe to do according to all that is written therein: for then thou shalt make thy way prosperous, and then thou shalt have good success.*"

The Bible is not a book for the casual reader, it is a book to be read, a book to be studied, a book to muse and meditate upon. It is a book to be loved, respected, and obeyed to the letter. Then and only then will it open to you and bless you beyond measure. Let the Word of God be a fire in your bones as it was to Jeremiah.

Jeremiah 20:9 "*Then I said, I will not make mention of him, nor speak any more in his name. But his word was in mine heart as a burning fire shut up in my bones, and I was weary with forbearing, and I could not stay."*

Problems with interpretation

As we begin our summary of the book of Revelation, please allow me to admonish you as to why there are so many different interpretations of the Revelation.

1. Many are hindered by <u>faulty teaching</u> from their past. All of us have been taught things throughout our lives that are not accurate. It can be difficult to move from a faulty position on things that we have been taught, but the student of Bible prophecy must "*prove all things*" with Scripture.

2. By not discerning the <u>literal from the symbolic</u>, many misinterpret the book. For example, the following Scripture is to be taken literally because the context does not lead us to look at it as symbolic.

Revelation 1:7 *"Behold, he cometh with clouds; and every eye shall see him, and they also which pierced him: and all kindreds of the earth shall wail because of him. Even so, Amen."*

In contrast, the following is obviously symbolic:
Revelation 1:14 *"His head and his hairs were white like wool, as white as snow; and his eyes were as a flame of fire...."*

This verse is symbolic because it says, "*like wool*" and "*as a flame*." The context of the scripture will help you discern whether it is literal or symbolic.

3. One of the biggest reasons is a lack of understanding of <u>parenthetical chapters</u>. By parenthetical, I mean a chapter inserted to explain something that has happened in the past, something that is coming in the future, or to further explain the present. It is like using a parenthesis in a sentence, only it is a whole passage or chapter instead of a few words. Let me

give an example of this principle in some Scriptures:

1 Peter 3:21 "*The like figure whereunto even baptism doth also now save us (not the putting away of the filth of the flesh, but the answer of a good conscience toward God,) by the resurrection of Jesus Christ....*"
Do you see the parenthesis used here? The sentence would make a complete thought without the words in parenthesis, but it makes more sense with those words included, as is the case with this next Scripture.

Revelation 2:9 "I *know thy works, and tribulation, and poverty, (but thou art rich) and I know the blasphemy of them which say they are Jews, and are not, but are the synagogue of Satan.*"

The book of Revelation is in order, but there are a number of "parenthetical chapters" inserted that will confuse if you are not aware of them. For instance, Chapter 7 is inserted between the sixth and seventh seals as a parenthetical chapter to explain some important details to the reader -- it is NOT in order. Chapter 12, a parenthetical chapter, begins 6,000 years ago at creation. It is important to know that portions of chapters 7,10,11,12,13, and 14, are inserted to further explain events, and are not in chronological order.

Basic facts about the book of Revelation

1. The human author is the Apostle John. He is the beloved, the one "*whom Jesus loveth.*" He was exiled on the Isle of Patmos for preaching Christ (Rev 1:9). As you study the lives of the great men God in the Bible, as well as those throughout history, you will find they were men that were going against the flow; men who were at war with the world's system. They used to say of Brother Lester Roloff, "You're rubbing the cat the wrong way." To which he replied, "Well, turn the cat around then!"

Persecution from the world is part of living for Christ. Friend, are you at peace or at war with this world?

2. <u>Revelation means to uncover, to unveil.</u> Just as a sculptor pulls the sheet off his work of art for an audience, the Book of Revelation is the unveiling of Jesus Christ, not John! Revelation 1:1 "*The Revelation of Jesus Christ, which God gave unto him, to shew unto his servants things which must shortly come to pass; and he sent and signified it by his angel unto his servant John....*"

The Book of Revelation literally shows us a side of Christ that we do not see in the Gospels. In the Gospels, we see him born in a lowly manger and riding on a donkey. In Revelation, we see him as King of Kings and Lord of Lords coming on a white horse with power and majesty and might! He came bringing mercy the first time, he is coming back the second time with wrath. The Psalmist certainly knew more than we realize when he said the following:

Psalm 2:12 "*Kiss the Son, lest he be angry, and ye perish from the way, when his wrath is kindled but a little. Blessed are all they that put their trust in him.*"

Friend, you must fall upon Him for mercy now, or one day He will fall upon you and grind you to powder. See what Jesus said here:

Matthew 21:44 "*And whosoever shall fall on this stone shall be broken: but on whomsoever it shall fall, it will grind him to powder.*"

The Revelation shows you a side of Christ that Hollywood won't show you, and--sad to say--most churches don't preach about.

3. <u>The book was written around A.D. 96.</u>

4. The theme of the book is the unveiling of Christ. One, who does not intimately know the Christ of Revelation, does not know Christ well.

5. The key verse and basic outline.
Revelation 1:19 *"Write the things which thou hast seen, and the things which are, and the things which shall be hereafter;*

*Chapter 1 explains "the things which thou hast seen."
*Chapters 2 and 3 explain "the things which are" in John's day.
*Chapters 4 thru 22 cover "the things which shall be hereafter."

6. A more detailed outline is as follows:
*Chapter 1: Intro, Christ and His relationship to His church
*Chapter 2 - 3: The Seven Churches - The Church Age
*Chapter 4: Rapture
*Chapter 5: Seven-Sealed Book
*Chapter 6 - 19: Seven Year Tribulation Period. (Daniel's 70th Week - Dan. 9:22-27)
*Chapter 20 - 22: One thousand-year Reign, Great White Throne Judgment, New Jerusalem

7. Take everything literally unless the passage indicates it is symbolic. This is very important to understanding Scripture. Phrases such as "*like as*," or "*as of a*," indicate the passage is *symbolic*, not literal.

Example:
Revelation 1:14 *"His head and his hairs were white like wool, as white as snow; and his eyes were as a flame of fire...."*

His hair was not "wool," but "white like wool." His eyes were not "fire," but bright "as a flame of fire." You will see this symbolism all through the Book of Revelation.

8. <u>God uses symbolisms to teach truth:</u>

a. Symbols are timeless. They have the same meaning and application in every generation and are not weakened by time. For example, a candlestick is used to represent the church in Chapters 1 - 3 as well as the two witnesses in Chapter 11. The candlestick is a type of light today just as it was in generations past. It is a timeless illustration or 'type.'

If the Lord had mentioned an F-16 fighter jet in Scripture, it would have meant nothing to the people of all the previous generations. Symbolic illustrations are easily understood in any age.

b. Symbolism interjects more emotion and feeling to the reader. This of course, separates the great novelist from the mediocre: the ability to captivate the reader.

Example:
God uses "beast" to describe the future world dictator we know as the Antichrist. This invokes much more emotional impact to the reader than to call him a 'one-world dictator.' It not only shows his position but shows that he is fierce and powerful and to be dreaded.

c. The use of symbolism requires study and perception to grasp. The lost man, as well as the casual reader, will not easily unlock its truths. We must diligently seek the truth. Remember, Jesus spoke mostly in parables to the people.

9. <u>The Book of Revelation is a book of sevens.</u> The word *seven* is found thirty-one times in the book of Revelation! Why? Because it is God's number of **completion**. The judgments played out during the tribulation are a series of sevens, and thus when done, is God's statement of **completion**:

1. Seven Seals
2. Seven Trumpets
3. Seven Thunders
4. Seven Vials or Bowls

I encourage you to consult a concordance to look up and read all the Scriptures concerning the sevens in Revelation. It is a delightful study!

The Book of Daniel: Additional prophetic insight

Daniel is an important book to study along with Revelation. In many Bible college classes, these two books are studied together. They describe the same end-time events from different perspectives.

For example, Nebuchadnezzar's vision in Daniel 2, Daniel's vision in Daniel 7, and the beast in Revelation 13, are all referring to the same concept but using different symbols.

The book of Revelation is filled with precious jewels for those who are willing to take the time to look for them. May the Lord grant you a bountiful supply!

"Behold, he cometh with clouds; and every eye shall see him, and they also which pierced him: and all kindreds of the earth shall wail because of him. Even so, Amen."

Revelation 1:7

Feasting with Jewels

In Leviticus 23, we find the seven feasts of the Lord. It is imperative to know that the nature of these feasts is as important to understanding prophecy as the jewels are to the working of a clock mainspring. These seven feasts are what I call **God's prophetic calendar**, and with a simple study of each, you'll be 'feasting' on the amazing and wonderful truths and the brilliant plan of redemption provided for each of us by a loving God.

In general, the feasts were given and ordained by God to be practiced by His people. They are mentioned throughout Scripture in both the Old and New Testament. In order to discern each feast's jewel, however, we must first examine the literal view, as recorded in Leviticus.

First Feast: PASSOVER

Leviticus 23:1-5

"[1]And the LORD spake unto Moses, saying, [2]Speak unto the children of Israel, and say unto them, Concerning the feasts of the

LORD, which ye shall proclaim to be holy convocations, even these are my feasts. [3]Six days shall work be done: but the seventh day is the sabbath of rest, an holy convocation; ye shall do no work therein: it is the sabbath of the LORD in all your dwellings. [4]These are the feasts of the LORD, even holy convocations, which ye shall proclaim in their seasons. [5]In the fourteenth day of the first month at even is the LORD'S passover."

Moses was given the instructions for the Passover back in Exodus 12. If you recall, the last of the ten plagues that God brought upon Egypt to free the children of Israel was the death of the firstborn of every family. Moses was instructed to tell the people to take a male lamb of the first year, a lamb without spot or blemish. This was to be done on the tenth of their month Abib. The lamb had to be watched for four days to be sure it was not sick. On the fourteenth day they were to kill the lamb and put the blood on the doorposts of the house. The blood would save the firstborn of the household. The figurative meaning is almost impossible to miss: the lamb represents Christ and His shed blood that saves us from death and Hell.

Second Feast: UNLEAVENED BREAD

Leviticus 23:6-8

"[6]And on the fifteenth day of the same month is the feast of unleavened bread unto the LORD: seven days ye must eat unleavened bread. [7]In the first day ye shall have an holy convocation: ye shall do no servile work therein. [8]But ye shall offer an offering made by fire unto the LORD seven days: in the seventh day is an holy convocation: ye shall do no servile work therein."

Exodus 12:15 *"Seven days shall ye eat unleavened bread; even the first day ye shall put away leaven out of your houses: for whosoever eateth leavened bread from the first day until the seventh day, that soul shall be cut off from Israel.*

God instructed that this Feast be started at the end of Passover

(15th) and continue until the 21st. For seven days the Jews could not eat anything that contained leaven. In fact, they had to remove all leaven from their homes. There were a couple reasons for this.

1. Leaven is a type of sin. After being delivered by the blood, we are to get sin (leaven) out of our lives.

2. They had to leave Egypt in great haste! There was no time to wait for the bread to raise, thus the unleavened bread. They ate the Passover meal in haste with their staffs in their hands ready to flee at any moment.

Exodus 12:11 *"And thus shall ye eat it; with your loins girded, your shoes on your feet, and your staff in your hand; and ye shall eat it in haste: it is the LORD'S passover."*

Third Feast: FIRSTFRUITS

Leviticus 23:9-*11*

"9And the LORD spake unto Moses, saying, 10Speak unto the children of Israel, and say unto them, When ye be come into the land which I give unto you, and shall reap the harvest thereof, then ye shall bring a sheaf of the firstfruits of your harvest unto the priest: 11And he shall wave the sheaf before the LORD, to be accepted for you: on the morrow after the sabbath the priest shall wave it

The Feast of Firstfruits was always the first day of the week (Sunday), after Passover. Literally, it was a time of offering the first-fruits of the barley harvest unto God in thanksgiving. This was during the barley harvest and took place during the Feast of Unleavened Bread, which lasted for seven days. A few other significant Biblical events occurred on this same day: the children of Israel crossed the Red Sea on this very day! In the New Testament, Christ arose from the grave on this same day!

Fourth Feast: PENTECOST

Leviticus 23:15-16

"[15]And ye shall count unto you from the morrow after the sabbath, from the day that ye brought the sheaf of the wave offering; seven sabbaths shall be complete: [16]Even unto the morrow after the seventh sabbath shall ye number fifty days; and ye shall offer a new meat offering unto the LORD."

Fifty days from the Feast of Firstfruits was the Feast of Pentecost. In Israel, the wheat was harvested at this time. In Acts 2, the church would be empowered with the Holy Spirit 1,500 years later on this very day. Pentecost is also called the Feast of Weeks. Also, on this date, Moses brought the Ten Commandments down from the mountain.

Fifth Feast: TRUMPETS

Leviticus 23:23-24

"[23]And the LORD spake unto Moses, saying, [24]Speak unto the children of Israel, saying, In the seventh month, in the first day of the month, shall ye have a sabbath, a memorial of blowing of trumpets, an holy convocation.

The Feast of Trumpets began at the new moon on day one of the month Tishri. The Jewish calendar is based on the moon. The Feast of Trumpets would be announced with the blowing of trumpets. The first of Tishri is in the fall of the year.

Sixth Feast: DAY OF ATONEMENT

Leviticus 23:26-27

"[26]And the LORD spake unto Moses, saying, [27]Also on the tenth day of this seventh month there shall be a day of atonement: it shall be an holy convocation unto you; and ye shall afflict your souls, and offer an offering made by fire unto the LORD."

The Jews call this sixth feast, Yom Kippur. It is their holiest day of the year. It is that one day of the year when the high priest goes into the Holy of Holies and offers a sacrifice for the nation of Israel. It is my opinion that Christ will come back to earth at the second coming on the Day of Atonement.

Seventh Feast: TABERNACLES
Leviticus 23:33-35

"33 And the LORD spake unto Moses, saying, 34 Speak unto the children of Israel, saying, The fifteenth day of this seventh month shall be the feast of tabernacles for seven days unto the LORD. 35 On the first day shall be an holy convocation: ye shall do no servile work therein."

This seventh and final feast takes place on the 15th of Tishri, just five days after the Day of Atonement. The Jews would all assemble together, put up their tents, and dwell in them for seven days. Sometimes it is called Feast of Booths. Tabernacle literally means, "To dwell with." God wants to tabernacle or "dwell" with us. I believe this feast is a type of the 1,000-year Millennium.

This chart lists the seven feasts

1. Feast of Passover	Abib/Nisan 10th - 14th (our March or April)
2. Feast of Unleavened Bread	Abib/Nisan 15th - 21st , 7 days
3. Feast of Firstfruits	First day of week after Passover
4. Feast of Pentecost	Fifty days after Firstfruits
Four Month Gap Here	
5. Feasts of Trumpets	1st day of Seventh Month
6. Feast of Day of Atonement	10th day of Seventh Month
7. Feast of Tabernacles	15th day of Seventh Month

A Few Observations

1. The seven feasts all take place in seven months

beginning in Abib and ending in Tishri. The number seven is God's number of completion.

2. The first four feasts are spring feasts and **have already been fulfilled** by Christ.
3. The last three feasts occur in the fall month of Tishri and are **yet to be fulfilled.**

God's Prophetic Calendar

The seven feasts are symbolic of future events. I call them God's prophetic calendar. The understanding of the prophetic nature of the seven feasts will help you see the world from God's perspective.

The seven feasts take place during the first seven months of the Jewish year. Seven is God's number of completion. I believe there will be 7,000 years of human history. There were six days of creation and God rested on the seventh day.

2 Peter 3:8 *"But, beloved, be not ignorant of this one thing, that one day is with the Lord as a thousand years, and a thousand years as one day.*"

The first four feasts symbolize events that have already taken place. However, let's remember that when they were given to Moses in Leviticus 23, they were prophetic of the coming of Messiah, which was a future event in Moses day. The last three feasts take place in the fall and are symbolic of events yet to come. **Christ fulfilled the first four feasts right to the exact day.** Isn't that amazing? Will the last three be fulfilled on their exact day? It is possible and in fact very probable since we know the Lord is a God of order.

Three Unfulfilled Feasts Heralded by a Trumpet Blast

The final three fall feasts begin with the blowing of a trumpet. They picture future events that have yet to be fulfilled. The next event on God's calendar is the rapture.

The Bible indicates that the rapture occurs with the blowing of trumpets.

1 Thessalonians 4:16-17 *"[16]For the Lord himself shall descend from heaven with a shout, with the voice of the archangel, and with the trump of God: and the dead in Christ shall rise first: "[17]Then we which are alive and remain shall be caught up together with them in the clouds, to meet the Lord in the air: and so shall we ever be with the Lord."*

Revelation 4:1 *"After this I looked, and, behold, a door was opened in heaven: and the first voice which I heard was as it were of a trumpet talking with me; which said, Come up hither, and I will shew thee things which must be hereafter."*

1 Corinthians 15:52 *"In a moment, in the twinkling of an eye, at the* <u>*last trump*</u>*: for* <u>*the trumpet shall sound*</u>*, and the dead shall be raised incorruptible, and we shall be changed."*

Feast of Trumpets - Prophetic of the rapture

1. It is the next feast of the seven, awaiting fulfillment, just as the rapture is the next event on God's timetable.
2. It is the one feast that no man knows the day or hour that it begins. It is the only feast that begins at the sighting of the new moon in the sky. It was then that the trumpet would be blown and the feast would officially begin.
3. It is the feast that fits the description of the rapture with the blowing of trumpets.
4. It is the beginning of fruit harvest. Likewise, the rapture is a harvest of the souls of men.

There are twenty-nine days in the Hebrew month of Elul, which is the month right before Tishri. In Bible days, the Jews would blow a trumpet each of these twenty-nine days looking forward to the 'last trump', which is the announcement of the Feast of Trumpets on Tishri 1. The Jews call the Feast of Trumpets "Rosh Hashanah" meaning head of the year. It is the New Year on their secular calendar.

Day of Atonement – The Second Coming of Christ

After the Feast of Trumpets comes the Day of Atonement. This is the sixth feast which the Jews call Yom Kippur. It is a most holy day for the Jews. It was the one time a year that the High Priest could enter the Holy of Holies and offer a sacrifice for the nation. I believe this sixth feast is prophetic of the Second Coming of Christ at the end of the Tribulation. This is where Christ stands on the Mount of Olives as was prophesied in the book of Acts.

Acts 1:11-12 *"[11]Which also said, Ye men of Galilee, why stand ye gazing up into heaven? this same Jesus, which is taken up from you into heaven, shall so come in like manner as ye have seen him go into heaven. [12]Then returned they unto Jerusalem from the mount called Olivet, which is from Jerusalem a sabbath day's journey."*

Tabernacle - Prophetic of the Kingdom Age

This is the last feast to be fulfilled. The people would gather and dwell in tents, sometimes called booths. This was five days after the Day of Atonement, and they would dwell there for seven days. It was a time of rest after the harvest. It is a type of the 1,000-year Sabbath rest called the Millennium. Shortly after returning to the Mount of Olives with the title deed to planet earth in His hand, Christ will set up His kingdom and rule for 1,000 years.

These last three feasts all take place in the seventh month, which is our September or October. It is the time of the fruit harvest; it is in the fall. The Lord is coming back. The seven feasts give us a very intimate prophetic look at future events. We are to be watching for Him.

Seventy Weeks With Jewels

Daniel 9 is considered the most important chapter in the entire Bible when studying prophecy. In almost every seminary curriculum the prophetic books of Daniel and Revelation are taught together. They are like peanut butter and jelly: can't have one without the other. Daniel 9 is the jewel of all prophecy chapters, but it is a challenge to grasp for many. It is filled with strange terms like "*weeks of years*" and "*cut off*" and has various time-lines and visions. Sadly, many preachers never teach on these verses because they have never taken the time to study them out. Please read carefully as I explain this passage in terms that you can understand. When you grasp this teaching, you'll understand the timeline of end-time events more clearly.

The Passage

Daniel 9:22-27

*"[22]And he informed me, and talked with me, and said, O
Daniel, I am now come forth to give thee skill and
understanding. [23]At the beginning of thy supplications the
commandment came forth, and I am come to shew thee; for
thou art greatly beloved: therefore understand the matter, and
consider the vision. [24]Seventy weeks are determined upon thy
people and upon thy holy city, to finish the transgression, and
to make an end of sins, and to make reconciliation for iniquity,
and to bring in everlasting righteousness, and to seal up the
vision and prophecy, and to anoint the most Holy. [25]Know
therefore and understand, that from the going forth of the
commandment to restore and to build Jerusalem unto the
Messiah the Prince shall be seven weeks, and threescore and
two weeks: the street shall be built again, and the wall, even in
troublous times. [26]And after threescore and two weeks shall
Messiah be cut off, but not for himself: and the people of the
prince that shall come shall destroy the city and the
sanctuary; and the end thereof shall be with a flood, and unto
the end of the war desolations are determined. [27]And he shall
confirm the covenant with many for one week: and in the
midst of the week he shall cause the sacrifice and the oblation
to cease, and for the overspreading of abominations he shall
make it desolate, even until the consummation, and that
determined shall be poured upon the desolate."*

The main theme: 70 weeks

These "weeks" are literally weeks of years as we see from the context. Each week represents seven years. Seventy weeks equals a total of 490 years. Remember, Jacob worked seven years for each of his wives. The Bible says in Genesis 29:27 "*fulfill her week,*" speaking of a seven-year period of time.

These weeks deal with Israel, not the Church

In verse 24, we see that "*Seventy weeks are determined upon thy people and upon thy holy city...*" The people are the Jews, and the holy city is Jerusalem. We need to get this settled right from the beginning. The Church is not the subject of these seventy weeks; *Israel is the subject of the seventy weeks*. The seventy weeks are determined upon Israel, not the church. It is important to understand this.

The purpose of the seventy weeks in verse 24

a. To finish the transgression
b. To make an end of sins
c. To make reconciliation
d. To bring in everlasting righteousness
e. To seal up the vision
f. To anoint the most Holy

Have you ever asked yourself why there needs to be the seven-year Tribulation? Well, right here is the answer! The Tribulation is the final week of the seventy weeks appointed upon Israel. **One of the mysteries to be uncovered later in the book is that the final 70th week finishes off the 6,000th year and ushers in the Kingdom.**

The purpose of all seventy weeks is to put a final end to sin, bring reconciliation, bring to fulfillment God's prophecy, bring in righteousness, anoint the Lord Jesus Christ as King of Kings and Lord of Lord's, and begin the reign of Christ during the 1,000-year Millennium. The seventy weeks is also about redeeming the earth. Man's spirit is redeemed at salvation; our bodies will be redeemed at the rapture, the main harvest. The earth will be redeemed during the Tribulation when the seven-sealed book, the title deed to the planet, is opened (Revelation 5:1). All these things are a part of the purpose of the seventy weeks of years and are for Israel.

Sixty-nine of seventy weeks have already been fulfilled

In verses 24-26 of the passage, we see this is true. The first seven weeks (49 years) took place in Ezra and Nehemiah at the building of the temple and the walls around the city.

Then the next sixty-two weeks (434 years) took place from the building of the wall in Nehemiah until Christ was "*cut off*" at Calvary. This leaves one week (seven years) yet to be fulfilled after all believers are raptured.

This can be challenging to understand, but the Lord breaks it up into stages. The first 49 years is before the wall in Nehemiah, the next 434 years is after the wall, and ends with Messiah riding into Jerusalem on the donkey just four days before Calvary.

Daniel's 70th week is yet to come

God's timeclock stopped for Israel when Christ was "*cut off*" and crucified at Calvary. One of the reasons we are so confused about the dating of the calendar today is because we mark the start of the New Testament at the *birth* of Christ, instead of at His *death*.

At the renting of the veil, the Church Age began. When we get to Revelation 4, all the saved will be removed and the Old Testament clock will begin ticking again to finish off the final seven years we call "Daniel's 70th week." The Church Age will be over. It was 483 years from the time the command came to restore and build Jerusalem, until Messiah is "*cut off*" to pay the sin debt of the world.

Have you ever wondered why the people were waiting for the Messiah to ride into Jerusalem on what we call Palm Sunday?

John 12:12-15 *"[12]On the next day much people that were come to the feast, when they heard that Jesus was coming to Jerusalem, [13]Took branches of palm trees, and went forth to meet him, and cried, Hosanna: Blessed is the King of Israel that cometh in the name of the Lord. [14]And Jesus, when he had found a young ass, sat thereon; as it is written, [15]Fear not, daughter of Sion: behold, thy King cometh, sitting on an ass's colt."*

It was prophesied right to the day when Messiah was to arrive,

483 years after the command to build the wall. Many of the women in Joseph's and Mary's day were hoping to be the chosen one, and many prophesied of His soon-appearing. They did not know the month or day He would be born, but they knew right to the day when the Messiah would enter.

The 70th week begins at the rapture in Revelation 4 and is in two 42-month periods

Daniel 9:27 *"And he shall confirm the covenant with many for one week: and in the midst of the week he shall cause the sacrifice and the oblation to cease, and for the overspreading of abominations he shall make it desolate, even until the consummation, and that determined shall be poured upon the desolate."*

This says that in the "midst" or "middle" of the week of seven years, the Antichrist shall enter the newly-built temple. (This temple shall be built before, or right after, the rapture and it may, in fact, be built for the Jews by the Antichrist himself.) He will end the Jewish sacrifices, declare he is God, and break the covenant.

Is there any question as to why the Dome of the Rock was built there? Do you understand why Jerusalem is such a hot spot in the world? It may be because the whole series of end-time events will consumate in that very spot! They have even put a cemetery in front of the Eastern Gate in hopes of keeping the Messiah from coming through! Matthew 24:15-24 gives reference to what Daniel spoke of and calls this second half of the 70th week the "*great tribulation.*"

Matthew 24:15-21 *"15 When ye therefore shall see the abomination of desolation, spoken of by Daniel the prophet, stand in the holy place, (whoso readeth, let him understand:) 16 Then let them which be in Judaea flee into the mountains: 17 Let him which is on the housetop not come down to take any thing out of his house:*
18 Neither let him which is in the field return back to take his clothes.
19 And woe unto them that are with child, and to them that give suck

in those days! [20]But pray ye that your flight be not in the winter, neither on the sabbath day: [21]For then shall be great tribulation, such as was not since the beginning of the world to this time, no, nor ever shall be.

Peace in the first half of the Tribulation

Israel will be at peace for the first half of the Tribulation. However, that peace will end when the Antichrist enters the temple in the "*midst of the week*"; declares he is God, and demands worship from Israel as their Messiah. All is well until the two witnesses, Moses and Elijah, left for dead in the street 3 ½ days earlier, come back to life and ascend back to Heaven in front of the 144,000 Jewish men who are assembled there for Passover. It is at that moment that they get saved and give glory to God!

Revelation 11:11-13 *"[11]And after three days and an half the Spirit of life from God entered into them, and they stood upon their feet; and great fear fell upon them which saw them. [12]And they heard a great voice from heaven saying unto them, Come up hither. And they ascended up to heaven in a cloud; and their enemies beheld them. [13]And the same hour was there a great earthquake, and the tenth part of the city fell, and in the earthquake were slain of men seven thousand: and the remnant were affrighted, and gave glory to the God of heaven."*

The Temple defiled

II Thessalonians 2:4 also speaks of the defiling of the temple at the middle of the Tribulation. "*Who opposeth and exalteth himself above all that is called God, or that is worshipped; so that he as God sitteth in the temple of God, shewing himself that he is God.*" This happens right at the middle of the Tribulation, in the "*midst of the week.*" The following passage is also applicable to this period of time we call the middle of the Tribulation. Scripture calls it the "*midst of the week.*"

Revelation 13:5-6 *"5And there was given unto him a mouth speaking great things and blasphemies; and power was given unto him to continue forty and two months. 6And he opened his mouth in blasphemy against God, to blaspheme his name, and his tabernacle, and them that dwell in heaven."*

Summary: Daniel 9 Prophetic Facts

1. The 70th week of Daniel 9 is the seven-year Tribulation.
2. The Tribulation (70th week) is for Israel.
3. The Tribulation (70th week) is NOT about the church.
4. Daniel's 70th week begins right after the rapture with the signing of the covenant with Israel. (Daniel 9:27)
5. The Tribulation (70th week) is in two equal parts.
   a. The first half is peace for Israel while the whole world is under a dictatorship and One World Order.
   b. The second half is the "time of Jacob's trouble" (Jeremiah 30:7), also called the Great Tribulation for Israel.
6. **Keep your eyes on Israel!**

There is one week left, and we call it the Tribulation!

A Jewel of Great Price

Several years ago I uncovered a shiny jewel from the Word of God that I had never seen before. What I found has proven to be a great truth in determining the timing of the rapture and has helped me understand the timing of end-time events. That 'jewel' surrounds the miracle of the birth of Christ 2,000 years ago. It is what I believe to be the greatest proof of the pre-Tribulation rapture! Let me share this jewel of great price with you as we close this part of the book.

Christ's first coming was a shadow of His Second Coming.

The first coming of Christ was in two stages: stage one was quiet and somewhat secret; the second stage was very public. He came first as a baby born in a manger. It was a very quiet event unknown to all but a few people. Thirty-three and one-half years later, He would ride into Jerusalem on a donkey and present Himself as their Messiah --- a public event that was prophesied in the books of Daniel and Zechariah. We call it Palm Sunday. On an interesting prophetic note, it was the 10th day of the month Abib, the same day the Jews would choose a lamb from their flocks to kill on Passover just four days later. **Jesus would become the Passover Lamb and it would be a public event before the whole world**. We can see clearly that Jesus came to the world 2,000 years ago in two stages: secretly as an infant to the Bethlehem manger, then publicly to Jerusalem as a grown man declaring the good news of salvation.

His Second Coming will also be in two stages.

According to Scriptures, when Jesus returns the second time, He will come in two stages, just as He did in the first. He is coming first secretly, to meet His Saints in the air at the rapture. Those remaining on Earth will not see Him. The rapture will be unexpected by most of the world, just as His birth was 2,000 years ago.

After the seven-year Tribulation, He will come back to Earth publicly on a white horse and ". . .*every eye shall see Him. . .*" (Revelation 19:11). That will be quite a public appearance!

This is a jewel of great price. Study if for yourself and I think you will find, like I did, how the simple story of Christ's birth is a shadow of a specific end-time event.

More shadows from Christ's birth on Earth

Yes, there are more shadows that point to the conditions of the world today as we await His second coming. The Christmas story we read each year in Luke 2 gives us an amazing prophetic 'heads-up'. As you read these shadows, I believe you will see that we fit perfectly as the last generation before the return of the Lord.

1. It was a time of tyrannical dictatorship. (Luke 2:1). Taxes, debt, and oppression were common. So too, are taxes, debt and social oppression major factors in our culture.

2. He came the first time to a place where there was no room for Him at the inn (Luke 2:7). He will soon return to a worldly people who have no place for Him in their hearts.

3. He came in the darkness of night (Luke 2:8). He is coming again into the darkness of sin and shame. He is coming to a church filled with fornication, adultery, and filth. He is coming to the church of the Laodiceans, one that has lost all boundaries and erased all lines of separation from the world. It is a big, one-size-fits-all, come as you are and be happy church---but *not* the Church of the Gospel!

4. He came to a generation that was "unaware" of His arrival (Matthew 2). When the wise men came to the temple looking for the King of the Jews, they found a people who were completely unaware. Likewise, I believe, the average child of God today is unaware of the lateness of the hour in which we live.

5. He came at a time of famine of the Word of God.

   Amos 8:11 *"Behold, the days come, saith the Lord GOD, that I will send a famine in the land, not a famine of bread, nor a thirst for water, but of hearing the words of the LORD:"*

   There were 400 silent years between Malachi and Matthew. Then God sent Jesus, the *living* Word of God, into the world. Friend, **today it is the same**. We have a famine of the *true* Word of God, as evidenced by the spiritual condition of the culture in which we live.

Observations

1. God communes with the humble. In Bethlehem, Jesus was not born in a palace; He was born in a primitive manger, among lowly shepherds.
2. Do not let the Lord find you unaware at His coming!
3. Get an urgency about the things of God and the return of Christ.

Upon further reflection....

When Christ came in that first stage as a baby, not much changed in the world. He walked the earth for thirty years before His ministry started, and almost nobody knew He was here. **I have a feeling that after the rapture, not many are going to be aware that we are even gone.** Apart from the terrible things that take place during the Tribulation, few will have any knowledge that the Lord has come.

It is later than you think!

This concludes Part One, I hope you gained insight into the Biblical jewels of prophecy.

In Part Two, you will be learning about Seven Ticking Clocks. I trust these clocks will reveal to you the lateness of the hour in which we live.

Part Two

The Seven Ticking Clocks

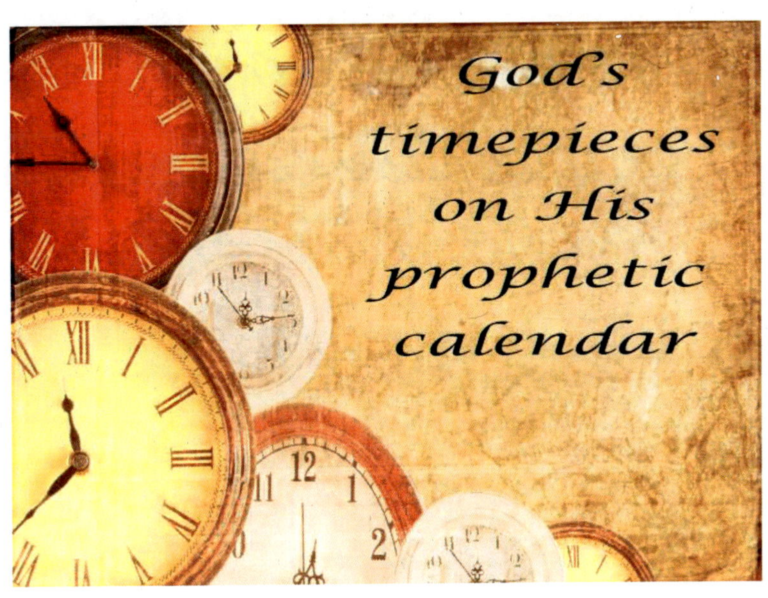

God's prophetic clock was pre-wound to tick for 6,000-years and today, we are living in its final hour!

The Ticking 6,000 Year Clock

The first and most basic "clock" is that of the 6000 years that God set forth in His plan for man here on earth. With the inundation of evolution, science, and biology based only on men's wisdom, we have been culturally programmed to think of our earth and human race as "millions and billions" of years old. That's not what the Bible says.

Here, you will be introduced to many Biblical truths, the main one being the world will last for 6,000 years, after which the Kingdom Age, another 1,000 years, will take place. That's a total of 7,000 years. Once again, seven is God's number of completion.

The 6,000-year clock is ticking down. I firmly believe we are very close to the end of this age.

Let's start in Genesis to see how these truths unfold. Keep in mind that from the very beginning, God was revealing to the faithful saints the timing of His events!

Genesis 1:1-5

"In the beginning God created the heaven and the earth. 2And the earth was without form, and void; and darkness was upon the face of the deep. And the Spirit of God moved upon the face of the waters. 3And God said, Let there be light: and there was light. 4And God saw the light, that it was good: and God divided the light from the darkness. 5And God called the light Day, and the darkness he called Night. And the evening and the morning were the first day."

The Creative Week

If you read from Genesis 1:1 to Chapter 2:2, God simply reveals how He created everything from nothing in six days, then rested on the seventh day. But take a closer look: these seven days of creation are prophetic of 7,000 years of human history on the earth. Each day represents 1,000 years. Just as creation was completed in six days, so too, human history will be completed in 6,000 years. The seventh day of rest is comparable to the 1,000-year Kingdom Age (also called the Millennium). At the point in history that you are reading this, we are very close to the end of the 6,000th year, and the clock is tickin' toward the beginning of the 7,000th year!

Scriptural Evidence

2 Peter 3:1-8 *"1This second epistle, beloved, I now write unto you; in both which I stir up your pure minds by way of remembrance: 2That ye may be mindful of the words which were spoken before by the holy prophets, and of the commandment of us the apostles of the Lord and Saviour: 3Knowing this first, that there shall come in the last days scoffers, walking after their own lusts, 4And saying, Where is the promise of his coming? for since the fathers fell asleep, all things continue as they were from the beginning of the creation. 5For this they willingly are ignorant of, that by the word of God the heavens were of old, and the earth standing out of the water and in the water: 6Whereby the world that*

then was, being overflowed with water, perished: [7]But the heavens and the earth, which are now, by the same word are kept in store, reserved unto fire against the day of judgment and perdition of ungodly men. [8]But, beloved, be not ignorant of this one thing, that ***one day is with the Lord as a thousand years, and a thousand years as one day****.*

In verse 1of this passage, Peter wants to stir us up by getting us to remember what was spoken of by the prophets and the apostles of the Lord Jesus as we see in verse 2. In verse 3, Peter says scoffers will be prevalent in the last days. We certainly have "scoffers" today. In verse 5, Peter says they are "*willingly ignorant*"! It is one thing to be ignorant, it is quite another to be "*willingly ignorant*". In other words, men choose to be ignorant of these prophetic truths.

In verses 5-7, he is speaking about the creative week of Genesis 1. In verse 8 he says, *"But, beloved, be not ignorant of this one thing, that one day is with the Lord as a thousand years, and a thousand years as one day."* Verses 10-13 go on to speak of the end of this world.

Consider for yourself: what could verse 8 possibly mean considering the laws of context and proper Bible interpretation? This Scripture is telling us **those seven days of creation are not only literal, but also prophetic of 1,000-year periods of time**. What else could it possibly mean?

Many throughout history have believed this Bible truth and written commentaries on it. Let me give you a few quotes from some men of old concerning a 7,000-year earth.

Wisdom from Past Generations

In 150 A.D., Irenaeus wrote in his book Against Heresies, "For the day of the Lord is as a thousand years; and in six days created things were completed; **it is evident, therefore, that they will come to an end in the sixth thousand years."**

In 300 A.D., Lactantius wrote this in his book Divine Institutions, "Because all the works of God were finished in six days, **it is necessary that the world should remain in this state six ages that is 6,000 years.** Because having finished the works, He rested on the seventh day and blessed it; it is necessary that at the end of the sixth thousandth year all wickedness should be abolished out of the earth and justice should reign for a thousand years."

In 1552 A. D., Bishop Latimer wrote, "**The world was ordained to endure, as all learned men affirm, 6,000 years.** Now of that number, there are passed 5,552 years [as of 1,552], so there is no more left but 448 years." (Till the year 2000)

Not only did men of old believe in a 6,000 year earth and then the Millennium, but look at the following Scriptures:

Hosea 6:1-2 *"Come, and let us return unto the LORD: for he hath torn, and he will heal us; he hath smitten, and he will bind us up. After two days will he revive us: in the third day he will raise us up, and we shall live in his sight."*

This is a passage dealing specifically with the nation of Israel. "*After two days*" is prophetic of the 2,000 years of the New Testament. *"The third day*" is the 1,000-year millennial reign of Christ, where Israel will once again be the center of attention here on earth. What else could it mean? These verses cannot be speaking of events that happen in three literal days.

There is more...

Psalm 90:4 *"For a thousand years in thy sight are but as yesterday when it is past, and as a watch in the night."*

Psalms 90:12 *"So teach us to number our days, that we may apply our hearts unto wisdom."*

NOTE: Moses is the author of this Psalm and will be one of the two witnesses during the Tribulation. That adds an interesting light on the context of the passage!

The Transfiguration Points to 6,000 Years

Let's look at the following Scriptures that suggest a 6,000-year prophetic view.

Matthew 17:1-9 *"[1]And <u>after six days</u> Jesus taketh Peter, James, and John his brother, and bringeth* ***them up into an high mountain apart****, [2]And was transfigured before them: and his face did shine as the sun, and his raiment was white as the light. [3]And, behold, there appeared unto them Moses and Elias talking with him. [4]Then answered Peter, and said unto Jesus, Lord, it is good for us to be here: if thou wilt, let us make here three tabernacles; one for thee, and one for Moses, and one for Elias. [5]While he yet spake, behold, a bright cloud overshadowed them: and behold a voice out of the cloud, which said, This is my beloved Son, in whom I am well pleased; hear ye him. [6]And when the disciples heard it, they fell on their face, and were sore afraid. [7]And Jesus came and touched them, and said, Arise, and be not afraid. [8]And when they had lifted up their eyes, they saw no man, save Jesus only. [9]And as they came down from the mountain, Jesus charged them, saying, Tell the vision to no man, until the Son of man be risen again from the dead."*

Here we have the story of the transfiguration. Remember, all Scripture has three interpretations: the literal, the figurative, and the prophetic. This is a literal event with an important prophetic lesson. Verse 1 says, *"And after six days. . ."* a shadow of Christ appearing after six prophetic days, which are 6,000 years according to 2 Peter 3:8. In the prophetic interpretation of this passage, we see Jesus coming in the clouds and showing His glory to the three disciples, a type of the rapture. If you are still not convinced, look at the last verse of the chapter before it.

Matthew 16:28 *"Verily I say unto you, There be some standing here, which shall not taste of death, till they see the Son of man coming in his kingdom."*

This verse teaches that some will not see death but will be translated. Then the very next verse, Matthew 17:1, *"And after six days. . ."* indicates a 6,000 year time span before the end. In verse 2, we see a type of the rapture of the church as Peter, James, and John are taken up into a mountain. In Matthew 17:3, the rapture occurs; Elijah and Moses come down to earth after the 6,000 years. They are the two witnesses who appear in Jerusalem after the rapture and are responsible for the conversion of the 144,000 Jews at the middle of the Tribulation.

This is an amazing prophetic story that gives us some interesting details about end-time events, but the main thing I want you to see is the 6 days/6,000 years lesson it teaches.

Moses and Elijah

As the Church goes up in the rapture, Moses and Elijah will come down to Jerusalem. They will preach to the Jews for 3-½ years. They will be hated of all men, yet; they will be the only light on the earth. They will be killed by the Antichrist right at the middle of the Tribulation and their bodies left in the streets for all to see. This will command worldwide media attention, and the entire population will rejoice that they are dead. The Bible says, after 3 ½ days, they come back to life and ascend to Heaven exactly as Jesus did, and on the same feast day that Jesus rose from the grave, the Feast of Firstfruits. I believe it is at this time that the 144,000 Jewish men will get saved. These men will be assembled in Jerusalem for Passover and will witness this event taking place.

(I teach more about this in my book titled *Revelation Study Guide*)

Prophetic application of the Transfiguration

Why the transfiguration and why did Moses and Elijah meet with Jesus? Here is what I believe. **I believe Moses and Elijah had to see Jesus Christ in His glorified body because they are coming back to be witnesses of the Messiah, during Daniel's 70th week.** You have to see or hear something to be a witness. It is possible they are the two men in white apparel at the tomb after the resurrection and the two men at the Ascension forty days later (Luke 24:4 and Acts 1:10).

(See my book *The Mystery of the Jubilee* for more on this subject.)

There were only three people in the Bible that fasted for forty days: Jesus, Moses, and Elijah; and they are all together at the transfiguration.

A Giant Sabbatical Cycle

When God rested on the seventh day, He set the precedent for the Sabbath rest that Jews practice to this day. If you think about it, the entire 7,000-year time-frame is actually a giant sabbatical cycle with the 1,000-year Kingdom Age represented by the Sabbath. Do you think there is any chance God is going to be late for His Sabbath rest after 6,000 years of history?

Hebrews 4:4 *"For he spake in a certain place of the seventh day on this wise, And God did rest the seventh day from all his works."*

Timing is important: Can we trust our calendar?

Sadly, we cannot trust either the Gregorian calendar or the Jewish calendar since both have been altered over the centuries. However, Jesus told us there would be signs that confirm we are in "the season." Currently, the signs indicate we are in the final season of the 6,000 years prophesied.

A Simple Timeline

The 6,000-year period consists of: 4,000 years (which includes Creation through the end of the Old Testament); plus 2,000 years of the New Testament. As simple as this math is, it is important to understand *when* the Old Testament ended, and the New Testament began.

33 ½ Year Mistake

Upon extensive study, we find that the Gregorian calendar we use records the New Testament starting at the incorrect time! In the Scofield Bible there is a date referenced at the top of each page. Bishop James Ussher, who is known for attempting to give us the historical, chronological timeline, gave us these dates back in the 1600's, but he erred greatly in this instance. He has the New Testament beginning at the birth of Christ. In fact, he has Jesus being born in 4 B.C. As a result, most of us were taught the New Testament started at the birth of Jesus Christ.

In truth, the New Testament started, not at the birth, but at the death of Christ. Since Jesus lived 33 ½ years, it becomes quite an issue when trying to figure out where we are on the 6,000-year clock. In fact, it leaves us with a 33½- year mistake to correct.

End of the Old Testament

Daniel 9:24-26 "[24]*Seventy weeks are determined upon thy people and upon thy holy city, to finish the transgression, and to make an end of sins, and to make reconciliation for iniquity, and to bring in everlasting righteousness, and to seal up the vision and prophecy, and to anoint the most Holy.* [25]*Know therefore and understand, that from the going forth of the commandment to restore and to build Jerusalem unto the*

Messiah the Prince shall be seven weeks, and threescore and two weeks: the street shall be built again, and the wall, even in troublous times. [26]And after threescore and two weeks shall ***Messiah be cut off****, but not for himself: and the people of the prince that shall come shall destroy the city and the sanctuary; and the end thereof shall be with a flood, and unto the end of the war desolations are determined."*

Notice what I underlined in these verses. The Bible clearly states that 70 weeks (490 years) are determined upon Israel. The 69th week, which was Old Testament, did not end at the birth of Christ, but at Calvary when Messiah was "*cut off*" as the text shows. As you can see in this passage, Daniel's 70th week (seven-year Tribulation) is also Old Testament! Daniel's 69 weeks (483 years) were ticking down from the time of Nehemiah until Christ was "*cut off*" at Calvary. The countdown ended at the death of Christ on the cross. When the New Testament Age ends at the rapture, Daniel's 70th week begins. The 70th week will fulfill the prophecy of Daniel 9, and complete the 4,000 years of the Old Testament. Why have scholars and theologians missed these simple truths? I think C.I. Scofield said it best in his introduction to The Revelation in the 1907 Scofield Reference Bible:

"Doubtless much which is designedly obscure to us will be clear to those for whom it was written as the time approaches."

When did the New Testament Begin?

As I stated previously, I believe the New Testament Age began not at the birth of Christ, but rather after His death. Let me give you several reasons why I strongly believe this. I already mentioned Messiah being "*cut off*" in Daniel 9 that signifies a gap between the 69th and 70th weeks. These 70 weeks are all Old Testament, but there is a gap between them that, we call the Church Age. It is the New Testament.

The Church is a parenthesis stuck in between the 69th and 70th week of Daniel.

Here are a few more examples of how the Scriptures indicate that the New Testament began *after* the death of Christ.

The Temple Veil

Matthew 27:50-51 "Jesus, when he had cried again with a loud voice, yielded up the ghost. And, behold, the veil of the temple was rent in twain from the top to the bottom; and the earth did quake, and the rocks rent;"

The veil in the temple was not rent in twain until *after* Jesus died. This veil was a separation between God and man. The veil sealed off the "Holy of Holies" that could only be entered once a year by the High Priest. This veil was no longer needed, and therefore rent in two, because Jesus who became our sacrifice, had just become our High Priest. At His death, Jesus cried out, "It is finished."

He was speaking of three things:

- **a.** His physical life.
- **b.** The payment for sin.
- **c.** The Old Testament Age.

The Death of Jesus, the Testator

Hebrews 9:15-17 *"15 And for this cause he is the mediator of the new testament, that by means of death, for the redemption of the transgressions that were under the first testament, they which are called might receive the promise of eternal inheritance. 16 For where a testament is, there must also of necessity be the death of the testator. 17 For a testament is of force after men are dead: otherwise it is of no strength at all while the testator liveth."*

If a man were to record his last will and testament at the courthouse, it is considered legal but not binding until his death. Christ is the Lamb slain from the foundation of the world. This was sealed in the foreknowledge of God. At the cross of Calvary, the Testator died for the sins of the world, and the New Testament Age began; again indicating that the New Testament could not have begun until after the death of Jesus Christ.

Webster's 1828 Dictionary

TESTA'TOR, n. [L.] A man who makes and leaves a will or testament at death.

TEST'AMENT, n. [L. testamentum, from testor, to make a will.]

1. A solemn authentic instrument in writing, by which a person declares his will as to the disposal of his estate and effects **after his death**. This is otherwise called a will. A testament, to be valid, must be made when the testator is of sound mind, and it must be subscribed, witnessed and published in such manner as the law prescribes. A man in certain cases may make a valid will by words only, and such "will" is called nuncupative.

The starting point of the New Testament is vital to understanding where we are on God's prophetic clock!

The Mystery of Time

Often, the Bible seems confusing or difficult to interpret when determining the timing of prophetic events. But don't be deceived or frustrated---God's Word is absolutely precise, and it reveals His plan as executed to the exact minute. Remember: *"It is the glory of God to conceal a thing, but the honour of kings is to* ***search out*** *a matter."* (Prov. 25:2)

Please allow me to share three different concepts that I believe will help you understand the perfect timing of these last days.

1. The Chess Clock.

Have you ever played chess? When I was in high school I was on the chess team that went to the Maine State High School Tournament. On tournament level, competitors always use a chess clock, like the one pictured.

Simply put, this double clock is used to time each player's move. To begin the match, the first clock is started. When player A completes his move, he stops his clock. This automatically starts player B's clock. Player B then makes his move, stops his clock and that triggers player A's clock to start again. **Only one clock can be ticking at a time.**

This is a great illustration of God's prophetic clock. As you can see in the picture, I labeled each clock: the left represents the Old Testament (O.T.), and the right represents the New Testament (N.T.). Later in this chapter, I will show you how this chess clock applies to prophetic events.

We know from earlier study of the days of creation in Genesis, God set forth 4,000 years on the Old Testament clock and 2,000 years on the New Testament clock. Again, this equals 6,000 years, added to the final 1,000-year Kingdom Age, the total is 7,000.

2. The 6,000-year timeline illustrated.
Please consider the two timelines. The first is a simple timeline while the second is a little more complex.

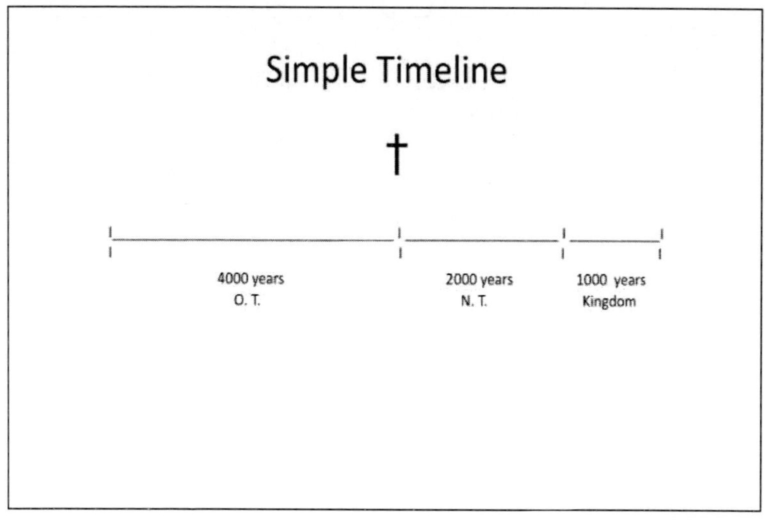

Simple enough, right? The chart shows the 4,000 years from creation to the cross and 2,000 years from the cross to the Kingdom Age. Well, all the numbers add up, but let's look at the second timeline, which I believe to be the actual one:

I believe the Old Testament ended at the year 3993, not the year 4000 as most people teach. The Tribulation is Old Testament and will finish off the seven missing years. Please take the time to consider the following:

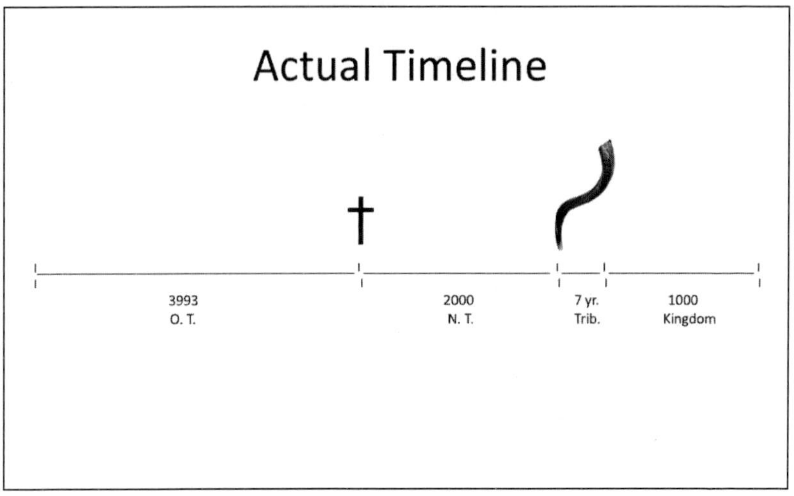

Daniel's 70 weeks (Daniel 9:24-27) are all Old Testament and concern Israel. When the Old Testament ended soon after Calvary, it was only the 69th week. That means *there is still another week of seven years of the Old Testament left to be fulfilled.* We call it the seven-year Tribulation period, but it is actually Daniel's 70th week.

The Church Age = A Parenthetical Period

The 2000-year Church Age is actually a parenthetical period that God inserted between the 69th and the 70th week of Daniel!

When the trumpet sounds at the rapture of the church, it will signal the end of the Church Age (NT), and begin the Tribulation which is the final seven years as prophesized in the Old Testament!

Using the illustration of the chess clock, God 'stopped' the Old Testament clock and the New Testament clock began. Not a second was missed! Now, 2000 years later, when the church is to be raptured, at that moment the New Testament clock will be stopped, and the Old Testament clock will begin again---it will not miss a single second! Daniel's 70th week will tick down for the final seven year, after which the 1,000-year Kingdom Age will be ushered in.

Amazing!

What's more, this is another proof for a pre-Tribulation rapture, as there is absolutely no way the church can be here for the Old Testament 70th week!

3. Stephen's role in God's prophetic timeline.

In the New Testament, Stephen, who may seem an insignificant Biblical character, actually illustrates a crucial importance to the 6,000-year clock. How? I believe Stephen was the *last prophet* sent to warn the leaders of the house of Israel to repent. Remember, Stephen was a believer and was ordained by the laying on of hands, but his ministry was cut short: he was accused of blasphemy (Acts 6:11) and brought before the council to defend himself. The council was angered by Stephen's testimony and stoned him to death.

As minor as his story seems, it is a significant piece of the prophetic puzzle.

Acts 7:54-59 "[54]*When they heard these things, they were cut to the heart, and they gnashed on him with their teeth.* [55]*But he, being full of the Holy Ghost, looked up stedfastly into heaven, and saw the glory of God, and Jesus standing on the right hand of God,* [56]*And said, Behold, I see the heavens opened, and <u>the Son of man standing on the right hand of God</u>.* [57]*Then they cried out with a loud voice, and stopped their ears, and ran upon him with one accord,* [58]*And cast him out of the city, and stoned him: and the witnesses laid down their clothes at a young man's feet, whose name was*

Saul. [56]*And they stoned Stephen, calling upon God, and saying, Lord Jesus, receive my spirit.*

First, I propose to you that Stephen died at exactly 6:00 PM, on the Feast of Trumpets at the end of a Sabbatical year just 6 ½ months after Calvary.

Secondly, Jesus died at Passover on the 14th of the month Abib/Nisan. The New Year in Israel is the Feast of Trumpets on Tishri 1. That means Stephen had to die between Passover and Trumpets and lived no more than 6 ½ months past the cross.

The Mystery of Stephen Revealed!

Consider these facts:

- Josephus, the famous Jewish historian who died in 100 A.D., wrote that Stephen and Jesus both died in the same year.
- Bishop Ussher, the man who gave us the dates used in the Scofield Bible, shows Stephen and Jesus both dying in the same year of 33 A.D.

- The Jews believe that creation began on Tishri 1 in the fall at 6:00 PM.
- A Sabbatical cycle is seven years long and ends not on Passover, but rather Tishri 1 (6:00 PM).

I believe it is highly possible that **Stephen died at the sounding of the Feast of Trumpets on the 1st of Tishri in the year 3993, and at that exact moment the 2000-year Gentile Church Age is grafted in**. I know this is new territory for most of you but allow me to give you some reasons why I believe this.

Stephen is the spiritual veil that separates the Old and the New Testaments.

1. **Jesus died in the middle of a Sabbatical year.**

Jesus died in the 69th Sabbatical cycle, but not at the end of the cycle. Passover is in the month Abib/Nisan at the time of barley harvest.

The end of the Sabbatical cycle is 6 ½ months after Passover at the Feast of Trumpets in the fall. When Jesus died on the cross, the veil in the temple was rent in two. This signified that all ceremonial law had been fulfilled. Jesus died in Abib/Nisan, but the end of the cycle is in the fall. **This means the 69th cycle did not end at the cross, but on the Feast of Trumpets!**

The ceremonial law as dictated in the Old Testament was ended at the renting of the veil when Jesus died, *but* the Sabbatical cycle does not end until Tishri 1. Everything changed after Stephen died.

I believe Stephen died on that very day and at the exact moment of the Feast of Trumpets.

Ceremonial laws were fulfilled by Christ at Passover, but the door was still open for the Jewish nation to head up the Church Age. The entire church was comprised of only Jews until after the death of Stephen. This is a fact that many Bible teachers have missed.

The Church was a Jewish church until Acts 10.

Stephen was the last to preach to the leaders of the house of Israel. I believe that Israel was supposed to continue heading up the church as they had been doing since Jesus ordained the Apostles. At the Feast of Trumpets in the year 3993, the door for the nation of Israel slammed shut and Jesus sat down at the right hand of the Father, thus officially beginning the 2,000-year Gentile Church Age! There was always going to be a 2,000-year Church Age, but I believe the Jews were going to head it up.

2. After the cross, the disciples were only preaching to the Jews. In Acts 2, the 3,000 added to the Lord were all Jews. The 5,000 who believed in Acts 4 were all Jews. The seven men chosen and ordained in Acts 6 were all Jews. Stephen was one of those seven men.

3. A strange thing happened at Stephen's death. In Acts 7, Stephen began his defense with a history lesson of the Jews. He started where it all began, with Abraham. He ended with Moses, David, and Solomon. Stephen showed them that history all pointed to Jesus Christ and that they were "*...stiffnecked and uncircumcised in heart and ears...*"

Stephen rebuked them for their unbelief! They picked up stones and killed the messenger from God. When Stephen was dying, he looked up to Heaven and saw Jesus "*...**standing** on the right hand of God.*" In Paul's writings, we read that Jesus is "*...**seated** at the right hand of the Father.*" Jesus had not taken His seat at the right hand of the Father before Stephen died. The door was still open to the Jews to accept Him and become head of the Church Age!

Once again, in short, Stephen was the last Old Testament prophet to preach to the nation of Israel that Christ was/is the Messiah. When they rejected the message of Stephen, Jesus sat down, and **the door closed on Israel and has been closed for 2,000 years**. Let me be clear, Jews can and are being saved, but as a nation they have been put on the back burner. As a nation, they are not involved in the work of the church as they could have been, but one of these days the Jews will rise again and fulfill their role during the last days.

4. After Stephen died, everything changed. Saul (later called Paul), was the one holding the garments of those who stoned Stephen. It is he that God would touch in Acts 9 and be called to go unto the Gentiles. When you get to Acts 10, you have the Gentile household of Cornelius getting saved. Remember the Lord said, "...*What God hath cleansed, that call not thou common.*" (Acts 10:15). Peter understood the vision of the unclean beasts meant God was going to use the Gentiles as the church!

It bears repeating: *After Stephen died, everything changed!* Paul got saved in Acts 9 and he would become the Apostle unto the Gentiles. The Gentile church is grafted in and begins to carry the Gospel around the world. What God intended for his chosen people, the Jews to continue, became the calling of the Gentile church.

Closing Summary

* It is possible that Stephen died at the end of the 69th Sabbatical cycle on Tishri 1, at 6:00 PM in the year 3993, right to the second on the Old Testament clock!

* He was the last prophet to warn and exhort the leaders of Israel to repent.

I realize that some of this is speculation and that we cannot be sure of the scenario I am sharing with you. Consider my final thoughts concerning this theory as it contributes to the revelations of the 6,000-year clock, God's Sabbatical teachings, and Daniel's prophecies.

On Feast of Trumpets, the door slammed shut for Israel, and the Church Age clock began ticking at the year 3993. It has been nearly 2,000 years now. Soon, God will declare that the nation of Israel is ready. God will announce in Heaven that it is Abib. (see more in the chapter on the Harvest Clock)

On God's calendar, seven months to the day from the new moon of Abib, there will be the sounding of the trumpet in Heaven. Jesus will come to earth to catch away His bride. He will come secretly in the clouds and the church will be removed. The trumpet sounding will be at the *exact moment* that Stephen died 2,000 years ago, on a new moon in the fall.

The New Testament clock will stop, and the Old Testament clock will resume ticking again exactly where it paused with the death of Stephen. Not a second will be missed. The seven-year Tribulation will take place while the saints are in Heaven at the marriage supper.

At the end of the 70th week, the Lord Jesus will come back on a white horse, with the "title deed" in His hand. The saints will be with Him. He will end the battle of Armageddon in an instant. He will come to the Mount of Olives and ride into Jerusalem through the Eastern Gate on the Day of Atonement on the 70th Jubilee and set up the Kingdom.

This will complete an exact 6,000 years of human history ... right to the second! May the Lord find us watching when He returns!

God's prophetic clock was pre-wound to tick for 6000-years and today, we are living in its final hour!

The Ticking Jubilee Clock

Another clock that every end-time believer should be aware of concerns the Jubilee. Like the 6,000-year clock, the Jubilee clock is counting down the time and is close to its end.

Simply put, the Jubilee marks a 50-year period, as defined by the Old Testament Book of Leviticus, in which the Lord declares a type of 'reset' for everyone in the 50th year. As will soon be revealed, much of Bible prophecy is connected to the Jubilee. We are approaching the 70th Jubilee from the time of Moses, and the 120th from Adam. I personally believe that it will be the final Jubilee and it is a ticking clock that is getting ready to strike midnight!

Let's get right to what the Bible teaches about the Jubilee:

Leviticus 25:8-13 *"And thou shalt number seven sabbaths of years unto thee, seven times seven years; and the space of the seven sabbaths of years shall be unto thee forty and nine years. 9Then shalt thou cause the trumpet of the jubile to sound on the tenth day of the seventh month, in the day of atonement shall ye make the trumpet sound throughout all your land. 10And ye shall hallow the fiftieth year, and proclaim liberty throughout all the land unto all the inhabitants thereof: it shall be a jubile unto you; and ye shall return every man unto his possession, and ye shall return every man unto his family. 11A jubile shall that fiftieth year be unto you: ye shall not sow, neither reap that which groweth of itself in it, nor gather the grapes in it of thy vine undressed. 12For it is the jubile; it shall be holy unto you: ye shall eat the increase thereof out of the field. 13In the year of this jubile ye shall return every man unto his possession."*

The entire 25th Chapter of Leviticus is a discourse on the Jubilee. Verses 1-7 explain the seven-year cycle of the Sabbath of the land (that is, six years of use and one year of rest); the remaining verses explain the Jubilee as being seven *times* seven Sabbaths.

Once again, the Lord points us towards the seventh day, which is the Sabbath. It is a prophetic concept, relevant to end-time study. **To review: God created for six days and rested on the seventh. Those seven days represent 7,000 years of history. The world will endure for 6,000 years and then rest for 1,000 years. This rest is called the Millennium.**

Why the Rest?

The Sabbath rest is because.... God wants to dwell with man! This is and was the plan from the beginning. *God wants to dwell with man.* That is what 'tabernacle' means; to dwell with God.

The Sabbath rest is also the central theme to the establishment of the seven feasts. For example, the Feast of Tabernacles is about God and man dwelling together in sweet fellowship. **The seven feasts are so important to understanding it all. They are the keys that unlock the door to prophecy. They demonstrate God's prophetic calendar.**

How the Seven Feasts apply

The seven feasts as described in Leviticus 23 were discussed in Part One, **but the Jubilee is intertwined with the feasts, and so makes further clarification of them necessary.**
The seven feasts take place within the first seven months of the Jewish religious year, from the months Abib/Nisan to Tishri. (There's that number seven again---God's number of completion!)

Note again how four of the seven feasts have already been fulfilled *to the day* by Jesus:

*On the Feast of Passover, Christ went to the cross and died. He was the Passover Lamb. He paid our sin debt during the full moon on Passover, the 14th of Abib/Nisan.

*Jesus lay in the grave on the second feast, the Feast of Unleavened Bread, proving there was no leaven or sin in His body.

*On the Feast of Firstfruits, Christ arose from the grave victorious over sin and death.

*On the Feast of Pentecost, the fourth feast, Christ empowered the church in Acts 2 to sow the seed of the Word of God.

Each of these four feasts were prophetic of the earthly ministry of Christ. Since that's true, what significant events do we have to look forward to for the fulfillment of the last three?

The three remaining, unfulfilled feasts occur in the fall and take place, according to Scriptures, in the seventh month of Tishri. Tishri is in late September or early October on our solar calendar.

The next feast yet to be fulfilled on the calendar is Feast of Trumpets. The Jews call it Rosh Hashanah. It is on the new moon which is the first day of their month. It is also their New Year's Day. *This feast will be fulfilled when the trumpet blows and we are caught up in the clouds to be with the Lord.*

Will it happen on the actual Feast of Trumpets on the Jewish calendar? The Gregorian calendar? There is no way to truly know because both have been altered throughout the centuries.

What We Can Be Sure Of

Seven years after the Saints are raptured on a Feast of Trumpets, Jesus will come back on the Feast of Day of Atonement to end the battle of Armageddon and put down the Antichrist (Revelation 19:11). In fact, you and I if we have trusted Christ, will be with Him. It will be a great day!

The final feast fulfillment takes place five days after Day of Atonement. This is the Feast of Tabernacles and will be fulfilled by the setting up of the Kingdom of our Lord Jesus Christ and the beginning of the 1,000-year reign we call the Millennium. It is the symbolic seventh day of the creative week in Genesis 1, and of the Lord's Sabbath rest. That is it! You now have the whole history of the world in a nutshell.

What does it all mean?

It is a beautiful, well-laid story of love and redemption. God created man to fellowship with Him, to tabernacle with Him. Man sinned and broke that fellowship. Passover, Unleavened Bread, and Firstfruits are God's plan to redeem man and restore this fellowship.

Pentecost is Christ empowering the church to go out and get people saved, which brings in more folks to fellowship with God. The Feast of Trumpets is the main harvest. It is the Bridegroom coming for His bride! We then have a seven-day wedding celebration in Heaven, while the Tribulation is going on down here on the earth. Then we come back with the Bridegroom on white horses on the Day of Atonement, and Jesus sets up the 1,000-year Kingdom Age where we will live and reign with the Lord.

Three Main Sabbaths

To fully appreciate this *ticking clock*, that I call God's final Jubilee, we need to understand it pertains to one of three main Sabbaths mentioned in the Bible. Let's look at them here:

1. The <u>seventh day</u> of the week is a Sabbath.

Exodus 20:8-11 *"**8**Remember the sabbath day, to keep it holy. **9**Six days shalt thou labour, and do all thy work: **10**But the seventh day is the sabbath of the LORD thy God: in it thou shalt not do any work, thou, nor thy son, nor thy daughter, thy manservant, nor thy maidservant, nor thy cattle, nor thy stranger that is within thy gates: **11**For in six days the LORD made heaven and earth, the sea, and all that in them is, and rested the seventh day: wherefore the LORD blessed the sabbath day, and hallowed it."*

The seventh day of creation in Genesis 1 was a Sabbath. God rested on the seventh day. He set a precedent way back in the beginning. In Exodus 20, Moses instituted the Sabbath. It is a day for man to rest from all his labors. It is also figurative. For instance, in the book of Numbers a man was put to death for picking up sticks on the Sabbath. <u>The Sabbath is a picture of resting completely in Christ for our salvation.</u> Picking up sticks was a type of working and not fully trusting in Messiah for salvation.

2. The <u>seventh year</u> is a Sabbath.

Leviticus 25:2-4 *"[2]Speak unto the children of Israel, and say unto them, When ye come into the land which I give you, then shall the land keep a sabbath unto the LORD. [3]Six years thou shalt sow thy field, and six years thou shalt prune thy vineyard, and gather in the fruit thereof; [4]But in the seventh year shall be a sabbath of rest unto the land, a sabbath for the LORD: thou shalt neither sow thy field, nor prune thy vineyard."*

According to Deuteronomy 15, all bond-servants were set free and all debt was forgiven every seventh year of the Sabbatical cycle. Also they let the land rest by not sowing their fields. They were to live off the double harvest from the prior year. God ordained that in the sixth year they would harvest twice the number of crops. The people had to trust in the Lord to operate under this system. It was a time to honor God and give thanks for His blessings. Interestingly, this is the Sabbath the people of Israel had broken which subsequently brought about the 70-year captivity in Babylon. God's judgment for not keeping His Sabbath was quite severe.

2 Chronicles 36:20-21 "[20]And them that had escaped from the sword carried he away to Babylon; where they were servants to him and his sons until the reign of the kingdom of Persia: [21]To fulfil the word of the LORD by the mouth of Jeremiah, until the land had enjoyed her sabbaths: for as long as she lay desolate she kept sabbath, to fulfil threescore and ten years."

3. The <u>49th year</u> is a Sabbath called the Jubilee.

Leviticus 25:8-9 *"[8]And thou shalt number seven sabbaths of years unto thee, seven times seven years; and the space of the seven sabbaths of years shall be unto thee forty and nine years. [9]Then shalt thou cause the trumpet of the jubile to sound on the tenth day of the seventh month, in the day of atonement shall ye make the trumpet sound throughout all your land."*

Every seven Sabbatical cycles (49 years) was a Jubilee, a proclamation of liberty throughout the land. On that day, a trumpet sounded and the whole 50th year was proclaimed as a Jubilee. God instituted three events to happen during this year, and when they are examined, you'll see why prophetically the Jubilee points to a ticking clock. Let's examine those three things here:

a. All debt was forgiven.

b. All bond slaves were set free.

c. All property went back to the original owner.

Leviticus 25:13 *"In the year of this jubile ye shall return every man unto his possession."*

This is how the Lord kept the land in the possession of the original twelve tribes of Israel as appointed under Joshua. According to Leviticus 25, the Jubilee is begun at the end of the 49th year *on the Day of Atonement*, the sixth feast!

Leviticus 25:9 *"Then shalt thou cause the trumpet of the jubile to sound on the tenth day of the seventh month, in the day of atonement shall ye make the trumpet sound throughout all your land."*

The trumpet is sounded and the entire 50th year is a Jubilee. Prophetically, the Day of Atonement is the day Christ returns to the earth on the white horse at the end of the Tribulation, puts down the Antichrist, and liberates the earth.

Revelation 19:11-16 *"11 And I saw heaven opened, and behold a white horse; and he that sat upon him was called Faithful and True, and in righteousness he doth judge and make war.*
12 His eyes were as a flame of fire, and on his head were many crowns; and he had a name written, that no man knew, but he

himself. [13]*And he was clothed with a vesture dipped in blood: and his name is called The Word of God.* [14]*And the armies which were in heaven followed him upon white horses, clothed in fine linen, white and clean.* [15]*And out of his mouth goeth a sharp sword, that with it he should smite the nations: and he shall rule them with a rod of iron: and he treadeth the winepress of the fierceness and wrath of Almighty God.* [16]*And he hath on his vesture and on his thigh a name written, KING OF KINGS, AND LORD OF LORDS."*

Since Christ is the original owner of the earth, I hope you see the significance of the Jubilee concerning the Second Coming!

Leviticus 25:23 "*The land shall not be sold for ever: for the land is mine; for ye are strangers and sojourners with me."*

Christ will fulfill the Day of Atonement and the final Jubilee at His Second Coming!

In Bible days in Israel, all property went back to the original owner every fifty years. As a Jew, if you sold your property or lost it due to debt, it was restored to you free and clear at the Jubilee. Obviously, anyone buying property in Israel in those days understood this and would have paid accordingly for it depending on how close they were from the next Jubilee. Basically, they were leasing the property. (Leviticus 25)

Now, these things are a prophetic picture of what Jesus has done for the sinner, and what He is coming to do at His second coming. *When we trust Christ for salvation, He sets us free from the penalty and payment of sin that we owe.*

It's about a Kingdom

The Jubilee is prophetic of Christ coming back to reclaim possession of a kingdom. God gave dominion of the planet to Adam. When Adam sinned, he forfeited that dominion to Satan, who became the god of this world and has legal ownership of the planet. This explains why he was able to offer the kingdoms of the world to Jesus.

Luke 4:5-7 "*And the devil, taking him up into an high mountain, shewed unto him all the kingdoms of the world in a moment of time. And the devil said unto him, All this power will I give thee, and the glory of them: for that is delivered unto me; and to whomsoever I will I give it. If thou therefore wilt worship me, all shall be thine.*

In Genesis 3, the earth was cursed when man sinned and it will be redeemed during the Tribulation. This is what the **seven-sealed book** in Revelation 5 is all about. Christ is the **Kinsman Redeemer** and will redeem the earth during the Tribulation. These two significant prophetic concepts are explained in detail in the following pages.

The seven-sealed book

The seven-sealed book is the key to understanding the entire book of Revelation and is crucial to our understanding of the Tribulation!

Revelation 5:1-7 "*And I saw in the right hand of him that sat on the throne a book written within and on the backside, sealed with seven seals. And I saw a strong angel proclaiming with a loud voice, Who is worthy to open the book, and to loose the seals thereof? And no man in heaven, nor in earth, neither under the earth, was able to open the book, neither to look thereon. And I wept much, because no man was found worthy to open and to read the book, neither to look thereon. And one of the elders saith unto me, Weep not: behold, the Lion of the tribe of Juda, the Root of David, hath prevailed to open the book, and to loose the seven seals thereof. And I beheld, and, lo, in the midst of the throne and of the four beasts, and in the midst of the elders, stood a Lamb as it had been slain, having seven horns and seven eyes, which are the seven Spirits of God sent forth into all the earth. And he came and took the book out of the right hand of him that sat upon the throne.*

This passage states that God the Father, the One sitting on the throne, holds a book in His right hand. This book is what I call the 'title deed' to the earth; a document that constitutes evidence of ownership.

Revelation 5 begins with a glimpse of One sitting on the throne with a sealed book in His hand.

You see, when God created the earth; he 'owned' it. He gave dominion of it to Adam, who sadly gave up the title to Satan when he and Eve sinned in the garden. Since that day, Satan became, and continues to be, the god of this world. However, our Heavenly Father has a plan to defeat Satan, and regain the title deed of the earth. It was planned since the very beginning!

Part of the purpose of the Tribulation period is to *redeem* the earth from the curse of sin.

Back in Genesis 3, a curse was placed upon the serpent, the ground (earth), and man. Man's soul is *redeemed* at Calvary (as soon as he trusts Christ), and his body shall be *redeemed* at the rapture, when all the the saints shall be raised incorruptible and receive glorified bodies (I Thessalonians 4:13-18 and I Corinthians 15:42-56). After the rapture, the earth shall be *redeemed* during the Tribulation, Daniel's 70th week (See Daniel 9:24, 12:4-9, and Isaiah 29:9-16).

This theme of redemption is further illustrated in Jesus.

Jesus is our Kinsman Redeemer

We see this in Revelation 5. Verse 2 asks, *"Who is worthy to open the book...?"* John weeps much because no man is found in Heaven or earth that is worthy to open the book. John is weeping for good reason, for if the book is not opened and the earth is not redeemed, the church cannot return to the earth for the 1,000-year reign of Christ, and Satan will be victorious. In verse 5, one of the twenty-four elders announce that someone has prevailed and is worthy to open the book. Who is it?

Revelation 5:5 *"And one of the elders saith unto me, Weep not: behold, the Lion of the tribe of Juda, the Root of David, hath prevailed to open the book, and to loose the seven seals thereof."*

The **only one worthy is the Lamb of God: Jesus Christ**! And, how interesting that the first time we see Jesus in John's vision of the rapture is here in Revelation 5 in the midst of the elders and the throne. The twenty-four elders are figurative (symbolic) of all the Saints gathered in Heaven at the rapture. We see the Father on the throne, the Holy Spirit, and Jesus. (We shall see Jesus on the throne in Revelation 20).

Revelation 5:7 "*And he came and took the book out of the right hand of him that sat upon the throne.*"

Jesus takes the book from the Father because He, and only He, meets the requirements of a redeemer, the Kinsman Redeemer. To fully understand Revelation 5 and this seven-sealed book, you need to understand the laws of the Kinsman Redeemer, and what could be redeemed. This is illustrated for us in the Old Testament.

Three things could be redeemed

1. Widow. The brother of a deceased husband was to take his brother's wife as his own. In the book of Ruth, Boaz is the kinsman who redeemed Naomi's land and took Ruth for his wife. Prophetically interpreted, Jesus is our Kinsman Redeemer, who 'buys' the Church with his own blood at Calvary and takes it for His Bride.

Acts 20:28 *"Take heed therefore unto yourselves, and to all the flock, over the which the Holy Ghost hath made you overseers, to feed the church of God, which he hath purchased with his own blood."*

Revelation 21:9 *"And there came unto me one of the seven angels which had the seven vials full of the seven last plagues, and talked with me, saying, Come hither, I will shew thee the bride, the Lamb's wife."*

2. Bond Slave. One who could not pay his debts became a bond slave to his creditor for up to six years. We, too, were slaves to sin, but Romans 6:1-14 tells us we are redeemed and do not have to be a slave to sin! In fact, the new man that has been born again -- your spirit -- *cannot* sin!

1 John 3:9 *"Whosoever is born of God doth not commit sin; for his seed remaineth in him: and he cannot sin, because he is born of God."*

Our old man, the flesh, still sins. It is the old man that we struggle with. This flesh shall be redeemed at the rapture. We will receive a glorified body when the trumpet sounds. So many get confused on this issue and claim that if we continue in sin, we are not saved. They will quote a verse like I John 3:9 to make their case. Yet the Bible clearly says in the same book, in *I John 1:8 "If we say that we have no sin, we deceive ourselves, and the truth is not in us."*

Is this a contradiction in the Bible? No, it is speaking of the new man, the born-again part, and not the old man, or the flesh.

Ephesians 4:22-24 *"That ye put off concerning the former conversation the old man, which is corrupt according to the deceitful lusts; [23]And be renewed in the spirit of your mind; [24]And that ye put on the new man, which after God is created in righteousness and true holiness."* (Also, Romans 6:6)

3. Land. This applies to land lost due to debt. The Bible teaches in Leviticus, the law of redemption concerning property or land. In the case of property, unlike a slave or a widow, when a person lost his property due to debt, a scroll was written up by the judges, and ownership of the land was transferred to the creditor. It was kind of like a bank repossession or foreclosure in our day. However, this was not a permanent transfer amongst the Israelites, as all land would go back to the original owner at the year of Jubilee. Inside the scroll would be the terms of redemption for the property. In other words, the cost of paying the tax debt or lien owed on the property. The scroll would then be sealed until one of three things occurred: a kinsman came to redeem the land, the debtor came up with the money owed, or the day of Jubilee, which occurred every forty-nine years. *The seal could only be broken by a person who met the qualifications of a kinsman.* This scroll is exactly what the book in Revelation 5 represents! It, too, is sealed, and it, too, contains the terms of redemption of property.

This scroll is the title deed of the earth, which is right now owned and controlled by Satan.

The book shall be opened

During the Tribulation, the seven-sealed book shall be opened and the terms of redemption of this sin-cursed world shall be redeemed in full by Christ, our Kinsman Redeemer. In Leviticus 25:1-55, we are given three qualifications of the one who could redeem property. This explains why none were found worthy in Heaven or on earth to open the book, except the Lord Jesus. Let us look at these three requirements that Christ alone fulfilled:

Requirements of the Kinsman Redeemer

1. He must be a near kinsman of the person who lost the property.

Revelation 5:5 "And one of the elders saith unto me, Weep not: behold, the Lion of the tribe of Juda, the Root of David, hath prevailed to open the book, and to loose the seven seals thereof."

Jesus fulfilled this role. He is of the right tribe and lineage. He was and is the only one who can!

2. He must be able to redeem the property.

The kinsman must have the financial ability to redeem the property. Praise the Lord, He owns *"...the cattle upon a thousand hills*." The Lord has the power and might to wrench this earth from the hands of Satan!

3. He must be willing to redeem the property.

The kinsman did not have to redeem the land if he did not choose to (Ruth 4:1-12). Praise the Lord, Jesus is both willing and able to redeem the land. For examples of the Kinsman Redeemer, see Jeremiah 32:6-15, and the book of Ruth, Chapters 1-4.

For nearly 6,000 years, this earth has been under the dominion of Satan, groaning and travailing under the curse of sin. The 6,000-year clock is ticking down; the trumpet is getting ready to sound. The final Jubilee clock is also ticking down. These two clocks are pointing to the exact same event, the redemption of the planet.

Searching Heaven & Earth

Revelation 5:4 *"And I wept much, because no man was found worthy to open and to read the book, neither to look thereon."*

In Revelation 5, we see the seven sealed book in the right hand of the Father. The book contains the terms of the redemption of this world. Heaven and earth were searched for one who was worthy, one who met the three requirements of the kinsman redeemer, and none was found. Now do you understand why John was weeping? He knew the following:

- **a.** If the book is not opened and the earth redeemed, all the Old Testament prophecies, yet to be fulfilled in the Millennium, will be void.
- **b.** All creation will remain under the curse. (Romans 8:22)
- **c.** Israel will never be restored. (Romans 11:1-36)
- **d.** Many Bible promises will be unfulfilled. God's word will not be true and God Himself would be proven a liar. (Matthew 5:18)

Praise the Lord, Jesus, our Kinsman Redeemer meets the conditions and is both willing and able to open the book and loose the seals thereof. There is great rejoicing in Heaven over this event.

The Tribulation is all about the redemption of the earth.

In Revelation 6 through 19, we see the awful terms required for the redemption of this earth from the hands of Satan and from the curse of sin. The entire Tribulation takes place from Revelation 6 through 19. Read again Daniel 9:24 and realize that the Tribulation is not about Christians nor has it anything to do with the church. The Tribulation is all about the redemption of the earth to make an end of sin, to make reconciliation, and to anoint the Lord Jesus as King of Kings! It is also God dealing with Israel. God has one final week of years to deal with them and to bring in everlasting righteousness.

Daniel 9:24 *"Seventy weeks are determined upon thy people and upon thy holy city, to finish the transgression, and to make an end of sins, and to make reconciliation for iniquity, and to bring in everlasting righteousness, and to seal up the vision and prophecy, and to anoint the most Holy."*

Observations to Consider

1. Weeping in Heaven

Revelation 5:4 *"And I wept much, because no man was found worthy to open and to read the book, neither to look thereon."*

You see, tears will not be wiped away until the end of the 1,000-year reign of Christ and the Great White Throne Judgment (Revelation 21:4). I wonder if there are some moms who weep in Heaven over a wayward child. Maybe a child in Heaven weeps over a lost parent. I do not think I have ever heard anyone preach about tears in Heaven, yet it is clear people can and do weep there. Tears are not wiped away until after the Great White Throne Judgment. I believe this wiping away of our tears is also a wiping away of all memory of our lost loved ones. I cannot prove this; it is just a theory of mine.

2. Prayer is important to God.

Revelation 5:8 "*And when he had taken the book, the four*

beasts and four and twenty elders fell down before the Lamb, having every one of them harps, and golden vials full of odours, which are the prayers of saints."

Our prayers are so important; God keeps them in vials, or bottles, for remembrance.

3. Singing is an important part of worship and praise.

Revelation 5:9 "*And they sung a new song, saying, Thou art worthy to take the book, and to open the seals thereof: for thou wast slain, and hast redeemed us to God by thy blood out of every kindred, and tongue, and people, and nation;"*

We should sing more often, and we should teach our children to sing. The Psalms were the hymnbook for the Israelites. "*Make a joyful noise unto the LORD. . ."* Singing opens our spirit to the filling of God's Spirit (Ephesians 5:19). I am afraid that the evil of Satan's music has crept into our homes and churches today and has opened our spirits to satanic influences

.

4. Since this world is not our home, we should lay up treasures in Heaven (Matthew 6:33). It is not our job to try to save the world, but to sow seed to rescue people out of the world. Only the Kinsman Redeemer can restore the earth.

This old world is sin-cursed. What a joy to know that one day soon, we are going to be "*caught up*" as John was, and we shall spend eternity with the Lord!

Now, getting back to the ticking Jubilee Clock…

The Second Coming of the Lord is a Jubilee

1. The prophetic meaning of the Jubilee.
Everything God set up has a purpose and a meaning. The

Jubilee fits the second coming of Christ perfectly! At the Jubilee, all debt is forgiven, all bond servants are made free, and all property goes back to the original owner. This is all fulfilled completely at the return of the Lord.

2. Time-wise we are approaching the 70th Jubilee.

There is that number seven again. Moses was given the instructions about the Jubilee approximately 1500 B.C. We will have 2,000 years in the New Testament Age. That makes 3,500 years total. Each Jubilee cycle is fifty years total. If you divide 3,500 by 50 you get 70 Jubilees. I realize Israel has not kept the Jubilee in hundreds of years, but I have no doubt that the Lord has kept up with it. After all, it is a Sabbath, right? God remembered the Sabbaths that the children of Israel profaned, and gave them 70 years of captivity in Babylon because of it. **The next Jubilee on the near horizon is the 70th.** Do you think that might be significant? I certainly think it is.

3. We are ALSO approaching the 120th Jubilee.

From the time of Adam until now, is 120 Jubilee periods of 50 years each. I realize that the Jubilee did not officially start until 1500 B.C. However, did you know that if you go back and start at Genesis 1 and count until the end of the 2,000th year of the New Testament, you get 6,000 years? If you divide 6,000 by 50 you get 120 Jubilee years. Is that interesting? Consider this passage of Scripture in light of that.

Genesis 6:3-4 "[3]*And the LORD said, My spirit shall not always strive with man, for that he also is flesh: <u>yet his days shall be an hundred and twenty years</u>. [4]There were giants in the earth in those days; and also after that, when the sons of God came in unto the daughters of men, and they bare children to them, the same became mighty men which were of old, men of renown.*"

We are not going to get into the discussion of whom the sons of God were. What I do want you to look at is the verse I underlined. Notice that God says man's days shall be 120 years. Most folks think that is talking about the years Noah spent building the ark. That is what I believed for many years. The problem is that it is not accurate. Truthfully, Noah spent no more than 100 years building the ark. We see here that Noah was 500 years of age when his children began to be born.

Genesis 5:32 "*And Noah was five hundred years old: and Noah begat Shem, Ham, and Japheth.*"

Genesis 6:9-14 *"9These are the generations of Noah: Noah was a just man and perfect in his generations, and Noah walked with God. 10And Noah begat three sons, Shem, Ham, and Japheth. 11The earth also was corrupt before God, and the earth was filled with violence. 12And God looked upon the earth, and, behold, it was corrupt; for all flesh had corrupted his way upon the earth. 13And God said unto Noah, The end of all flesh is come before me; for the earth is filled with violence through them; and, behold, I will destroy them with the earth. 14Make thee an ark of gopher wood; rooms shalt thou make in the ark, and shalt pitch it within and without with pitch."*

The command to build the ark was obviously given *after* Noah's three sons were born.

Genesis 7:6 "*And <u>Noah was six hundred years old</u> when the flood of waters was upon the earth.*"

Noah was commanded to build the ark *after* he was 500 years old and *after* his three sons were born. Then we see that the rains began when Noah was 600 old. That means *Noah was 100 years or less* building the ark.

Now, I pointed this out because we all have been given some

wrong teaching on the 100 years in Genesis 6:3, and I want to give you a theory about what I believe God is telling us in the passage.

It is my opinion that God is telling us that His Spirit is going to dwell with man upon the earth for 120 generations, and I believe a generation is 50 years. One hundred twenty generations of 50-year periods would be 6,000. If I am right about this, then God was saying that there will be 120 Jubilees making up 6,000 years, and then the end. My friend, the next Jubilee on the time clock of Heaven will be the 120th from Adam.

Jubilees from Genesis to Revelation

From creation to the end of the Tribulation is 6,000 years. There are 120 Jubilees in a 6,000-year period. I realize that the Jubilee did not officially start until 1500 B.C. with Moses. According to Genesis 6:3, it appears that God established the Jubilee to mark the whole history of man.

Second Coming and the Jubilee

At the final day when Christ comes back to the earth on the Day of Atonement, I believe it will be in a Jubilee year. Christ will have the seven-sealed book in His hand, and stand on the Mount of Olives. He will proclaim liberty, and will take back possession of the earth. That is what the Jubilee does, right? All property goes back to the original owner at the Jubilee. Hey, the Lord is the original owner of the earth!

Psalms 24:1 "*The earth is the LORD'S, and the fulness thereof; the world, and they that dwell therein.*"

Are we under the Sabbath?

In this chapter we have looked at the three main Sabbaths in the Bible. I think it would be good to end our discussion by explaining why we are not under these Sabbaths today.

In the time before the cross, these Sabbaths all pointed to

Christ. In the New Testament Age, the Sabbath is a shadow or a type of Christ and our resting in Him for salvation.

We do not keep the Sabbath today any more than we keep the ceremonial law of killing lambs for Passover.

And why do we not kill lambs at Passover? **Because the perfect Lamb of God fulfilled Passover, just as He fulfilled the Sabbath.**

Colossians 2:16-17 *"[16]Let no man therefore judge you in meat, or in drink, or in respect of an holyday, or of the new moon, or of the sabbath days: [17]Which are a shadow of things to come; but the body is of Christ."*

After Christ died on the cross, the veil of the temple was rent in two. The Old Testament ended and the New Covenant began.

Matthew 27:51 *"And, behold, the veil of the temple was rent in twain from the top to the bottom; and the earth did quake, and the rocks rent;"*

After the cross, the believers would assemble on the first day of the week instead of the sixth day. I believe this was just another sign from God that the Old Testament had ended.

John 20:19 *"Then the same day at evening, being the <u>first day of the week</u>, when the doors were shut where the disciples were assembled for fear of the Jews, came Jesus and stood in the midst, and saith unto them, Peace be unto you."*

Acts 20:7 *"And upon the <u>first day of the week</u>, when the disciples came together to break bread, Paul preached unto them, ready to depart on the morrow; and continued his* *speech until midnight."*

God did not put away the Old Testament laws; He fulfilled them.

Be sure you understand the difference. Christ was what all the lambs and sacrificial practices of the ceremonial law pointed to. He was/is the Lamb of God. These are wonderful principles and lessons for our edification, but we are not under the ceremonial laws of the Old Testament.

Matthew 5:17 *"Think not that I am come to destroy the law, or the prophets: I am not come to destroy, but to fulfil."*

Illustration

Let me give you an illustration that will help you understand why we do not keep the Sabbath or any other ceremonial laws today.

Imagine that you come to a prophecy conference and meet me in person, and I show you a photo of my family. That would be fine but imagine if my family is sitting just a few feet away! Wouldn't that be a little strange? Wouldn't it be better to just introduce you to them in person? You see, keeping a Sabbath or killing a lamb today would be just as silly. Those were figures and types to point us to the Christ who was yet to come. Since Christ has come, those things have been fulfilled, and we now can see clearly. *We do not need the types and figures anymore; we have the real thing!*

1 Corinthians 13:10 "But when that which is perfect is come, then that which is in part shall be done away."

The Church is A Ticking Clock

We are living in the final hours of the Church Age. It is a ticking clock that at first glance appears to be in over-time. However, as we learned in a previous chapter, the calendar was started at the wrong place. Though there is disagreement concerning when the church was founded, most agree that it was after Christ began His ministry at 30 years of age.

When the Church Began

Ephesians 2:20-22 *"And are built upon the foundation of the apostles and prophets, Jesus Christ himself being the chief corner stone; In whom all the building fitly framed together groweth unto an holy temple in the Lord: In whom ye also are builded together for an habitation of God through the Spirit."*

The church was started by Christ upon the foundation of the twelve Apostles. This can be looked at like the birth of a baby as Pastor Bill Waugh very elegantly explains:

"Christ is the head of the church that was started during His earthly ministry when He called out the twelve apostles. Christ is the Chief Cornerstone; the Apostles are the foundation, and we are built on them. Just as in a normal physical birth, the head appears first followed by the rest of the body. Christ the head appeared first, and the apostles and disciples followed. The rest of the church is built upon this foundation. A physical birth also includes a separation and cutting of the cord followed by the breath of life. Interestingly, after Christ paid the sin debt by dying for our sins, He ascended (separation) and the church breathed the breath of life (the Holy Spirit indwelling each believer) in the upper room and Pentecost. The church was clearly in existence several years before Calvary and the beginning of the New Testament Age."

Thus, we can conclude that it has been nearly 2,000 years since the church was founded. We are in the final days of the church; the clock is ticking down. I want you to consider the prophetic nature of the seven churches of Revelation 1-3.

The Seven Churches

Revelation 1:4 "*John to the seven churches which are in Asia: Grace be unto you, and peace, from him which is, and which was, and which is to come; and from the seven Spirits which are before his throne;*"

The seven churches mentioned in Revelation Chapters 2 and 3 are not only literal churches that existed in John's day, but prophetic of the entire Church Age.

Here are three reasons why I am certain of this:

1. The first verse of the Revelation shows that it is a prophetic book of things to come.

Revelation 1:1 *"The Revelation of Jesus Christ, which God gave unto him, to shew unto his servants things which must shortly come to pass; and he sent and signified it by his angel unto his servant John:"*

2. The chronological order of where the churches are mentioned in the book of Revelation. The rapture takes place in Chapter 4:1, right after the last of the seven churches are mentioned. The last church is a cold and dead church that the Bible indicates will exist at the rapture.

3. The character traits of all seven churches are clearly seen looking back on history as I've summarized below:

THE SEVEN AGES OF CHURCH HISTORY

The church of Ephesus – Desirable one/first - represents the Apostolic Age.

The church in Smyrna – Myrrh/suffering represents the age from 100-313 and Roman persecutions.

The church in Pergamos – marriage - represents the age from 313- 590 and Constantine united church with the state.

The church in Thyatira – continual sacrifice - represents the age from 590-1500 considered the Dark Ages.

The church in Sardis – remnant - represents the age from 1500-1700 with English Bible and reformation.

The church in Philadelphia – brotherly love - represents the age from 1700-1901 with two great awakenings and revivals.

The **church of the Laodiceans** – the rights of the people - covers 1901 until the rapture.

These dates are just approximate, but when you learn the meaning of the names of these seven churches as defined above, you find that they fit the time-lines given.

Today is the Laodicean Age, and is by far the worst of the seven churches. It started in the year 1901, the very year the Revised Version of the Bible came to America. Since this is the age that we are living in today, it is what will be the focus for the rest of this chapter.

Church of the Laodiceans

The church today has strayed from its foundations, much more than people realize. The *church of the Laodiceans* in Revelation 3 is a vivid description of the average church today. It is the final church as it exists right before the start of Daniel's 70th week.

It is not the age, but the spiritual condition of the church that is ticking towards end-time events.

The church that exists right before the rapture in Revelation 4:1 is the Church of the Laodiceans, as we see in the following passage.

Revelation 3:14-19 *And unto the angel of the church of the Laodiceans write; These things saith the Amen, the faithful and true witness, the beginning of the creation of God; I know thy works, that thou art neither cold nor hot: I would thou wert cold or hot. So then because thou art lukewarm, and neither cold nor hot, I will spue thee out of my mouth. Because thou sayest, I am rich, and increased with goods, and have need of nothing; and knowest not that thou art wretched, and miserable, and poor, and blind, and naked: I counsel thee to buy of me gold tried in the fire, that thou mayest be rich; and white raiment, that thou mayest be clothed, and that the shame of thy nakedness do not appear; and anoint thine eyes with eyesalve, that thou mayest see. As many as I love, I rebuke and chasten: be zealous therefore, and repent.*

Wait, did we just read a passage describing a future church, or was that a description of the churches on satellite television? To those of us with discernment, it is obvious that churches today fit the description in this passage. Yes, the church we just read about is here, now, and it is a ticking clock pointing towards the end of all things!

The church of the Laodiceans in Revelation 3 is a vivid description of the average church today.

Let's look at some characteristics of this church from Revelation 3:14-19 that will shed light on where we are today in relationship to this ticking clock.

Characteristics of the End-time Church

A group of people assembled at a park does not meet the Biblical definition of a church.

The church that Jesus founded is not just an assembly of people; it is a duly constituted body of believers set apart for God.

There are three pillars needed to set the church apart from the world. Without these pillars the church becomes just a place where people assemble. These three pillars are clearly pointed out in our text. The Laodiceans had lost all three of these important pillars. This passage is definitely prophetic of the final Church Age before Christ returns. In Revelation 3, we see three pillars that the Church of the Laodiceans lost:

1. It’s **soul**/identity.
2. Its **stand** for moral values.
3. Its hold on the **Scriptures.**

These three pillars are what separate a church from a club or a lodge. These three pillars are missing in the average church today - evidence that the clock is ticking down on the Church Age. This explains why Jesus is standing outside this church, knocking on the door.

Revelation 3:20 *Behold, I stand at the door, and knock: if any man hear my voice, and open the door, I will come in to him, and will sup with him, and he with me.*

The Church of the Laodiceans describes the condition of our average church today and is a ticking clock getting ready to strike midnight! Let’s look at these three pillars one at a time:

1. The final church loses its soul/identity.

By “soul” I mean they have lost their identity. Look again at the list of seven church ages on page 111.

The first six churches are called “the church **in** Ephesus,” “the church **in** Smyrna,” and so on. But look how this last church is addressed: it's refered to as the church **of** the Laodoceans.

Revelation 3:14 “*And unto the angel of <u>the church of the Laodiceans</u> write; These things saith the Amen, the faithful and true witness, the beginning of the creation of God;*”

This is the church that is prophetic of the last Church Age, the one we are living in now. The Lord seems to be revealing that the church has become a big all-inclusive universal assembly in the last days rather than a place for spirit-filled saints separated unto God.

The seventh church in Laodicea had changed; it lost the pillars that separate it from the world and make it unique. The people wanted to do their own thing; they wanted to exercise their rights. Not surprisingly, the word "Laodicea" means *the rights of the people.*

They lost their identity as a church and became just an assembly of people doing their own thing.

There was very little difference between the church and the world around them. What I just described would fit the description of most churches today. We are not separated; we are not different. We are no longer a "peculiar people." A lost person can visit on Sunday morning and feel right at home. We have lost our identity; we have lost our soul.

As I was writing this book I came across an article by Jan Markell that describes perfectly what this chapter is about. She even mentions the year 1900 as the start of the demise of the church.

What Happened to My Church

Jan Markell
Olive Tree Ministries

Church issues are the most frequent inquiry I get here at Olive Tree Ministries. Other leaders tell me the same. What has happened in the last 30-40 years? Many people visit church after church only to walk away disheartened. Others are lifetime members of a church and have seen changes that left it unrecognizable — spiritually speaking.

At first, members and attendees wonder if they are being a bit too judgmental, but the sad reality eventually sinks in that something has gone terribly wrong.
My background is in a fundamental church in Minneapolis that delivered verse-by-verse messages and had frequent prophecy conferences. Try to find that today! You will find a few but they are few and far between. This same church warned me about a coming apostasy back in the 1970s, but

who knew it would get so bad starting somewhere in the 1990s. *Nothing could have prepared me.*
First it was music that became the great divider. Nobody minds some guitars and a bass but into the second decade of the 21st Century, ear plugs are handed out as one enters the church sanctuary.

Some churches open with a secular song, dim the lights, add some smoky fog, and have an atmosphere similar to the local bar. All of this is to enhance choruses that will be sung two-dozen times by hypnotized church members. I would learn that it is to attract “seekers” — a 21st Century term. Bill Hybels admitted that he came up with the term but confessed it didn’t work well in his church!

Organs and pianos were tossed out 25 years ago because they did not promote “church growth.” The over-age 55 crowd was on their own. Some churches threw them a bone with an 8 a.m. service for those with gray heads. That trend began “the great divide” between generations.

Someone made a conscious decision that we should have a “new way of doing church”, although many members and attendees agreed *there was nothing wrong with old ways of doing church.* Terms began being used like “purpose-driven,” “seeker-sensitive,” “church-growth movement,” “postmodernism”, “Emergent”, and more.

People started to hear about love, unity and tolerance. We must be known for what we agree on, not what we disagree on. Everything and everyone must be accepted. Aberrations must be accepted. Sin must be accepted. People loved having their ears tickled. They would be encouraged to “feel good” and have their self-esteem built up. Sound doctrine was being set aside.
The saving of souls was being set aside for the entertainment factor and social justice causes. It seemed that many in the church no longer cared that so many were on their way to hell! What an offensive, intolerant thought. But clearly *sound doctrine will separate and divide so we must tread lightly in that area.*

Relevant issues have vanished. Pulpits have become afraid to talk about voting biblical values. Pastors quit speaking in favor of marriage and against abortion. It seemed like an “eleventh commandment” came into the church: *Thou shalt not offend.* *Taking a stand was clearly over.*

When it came to issues like Bible prophecy, the silence became deafening! People were told this was “divisive” although rock music in the church apparently was not! Millions are going to be left behind at the

Rapture of the Church but there are no warnings about this going out from hardly any church. Instead, pulpits are dispensing Osteen-type messages that talk about "your best life now" on this broken, corrupt planet.
This is just a short explanation as to why e-mails and letters pour into this ministry and others asking about how they might find a healthy, relevant church in their neighborhood.

In 2017 my friend Terry James invited me to submit a chapter in his proposed book titled "Deceivers: Exposing Evil Seducers & Their Last Days Deception." I had been doing Christian radio across the country for many years and as I researched programs, I was reminded daily that there had been a straying from sound doctrine.
I was confronted with the fact that I had two choices: I could overlook this trend or expose it. I took the warning to watchmen in Ezekiel 33 very seriously and I determined to confront the false teaching head-on and tell the truth about it. *I did not want the blood on my hands!* I knew this would cost me listeners and friends. I would soon find out that certain radio stations would marginalize me and even *ban me for the naming of names.*

Was this too high of a price to pay? I had to seriously ponder that and count the cost. Could I stick with my plan? It's a big, lonely world. We need all the support we can get. My plan would not win friends — but it might save some people from making lifelong theological mistakes by revealing who and what could be trusted and not trusted.

I began my research by tracing the history of false doctrine and reckless church movements going back to the early 1900s to the present. From mystical madness such as so-called Christian Yoga to the experiential of the New Apostolic Reformation, wolves were prowling around the flock.

At the same time, I saw that discernment was going over a cliff as books like "The Shack" and "Jesus Calling" were embraced as much as the Bible.

An entire movement sprang up around Todd Bentley who kicked sick people with his biker boot to heal them and this was celebrated.

Evangelical organizations like the NAE embraced global warming and called for America to destroy all her nukes. What does this have to do with the gospel?
Ecumenism soared, and Protestants began embracing Catholicism. Kenneth Copeland announced that the Reformation was over.

I observed something called the "laughing revival" and I concluded that it wasn't so funny.

I could go on and on. You can see that the odds of you having a healthy, well-balanced church are slim, but they are out there! If you have one, thank God for it daily. If you don't, know that you are not alone. Millions visit nearly every potential church in town and walk away perplexed and heart broken. Are they looking for perfection? A few may be, but most are not.

They just know today's church would most likely not be recognized by their parents or grandparents. Jesus said the gates of hell would not prevail against the church (Matt. 16:18). Having said that, the gates of hell are trying like crazy to penetrate the church, change it, change its message, change its purpose, distort the gospel, and wear down the saints — pastors included.

From September 05, 2018 Olivetreeviews.org

In this article, Sister Jan is exactly right. The church has lost its identity. We have lost our soul; we have become the Laodiceans!

2. The final church loses its stand on moral values.

We hear about how bad America has become, but I think the world around us is a mirror image of our churches today.

Revelation 3:16 *"So then because thou art lukewarm, and neither cold nor hot, I will spue thee out of my mouth."*

Preachers often blame the worldliness of their church on the influence of the world around him. I think it is the other way around.

The world around us is getting worse because the church has lost its influence on the world; we have lost our saltiness.

Matthew 5:13 *"Ye are the salt of the earth: but if the salt have lost his savour, wherewith shall it be salted? it is thenceforth good for nothing, but to be cast out, and to be trodden under foot of men."*

The leadership of our churches has begun to re-think who we are and what we stand for. Yes...I am talking about old fashioned standards and convictions! Many pastors today--and sad to say--many of them older men who have been in the ministry for many years, are having second thoughts about preaching on touchy issues that have separated the men from the boys for all these years! Touchy sermons like what's wrong with tattoos and warning the young folks about the evils of rock music. The churches of the prior generation were known for old-fashioned window-rattling, shingle-pulling preaching! Instead of church being a place to "reprove, rebuke and exhort," it has become an entertainment center for fun and games.

Instead of a place to be prepared for battle, the church has become a place for movies and sing-alongs and casual fellowship!

We no longer preach the dangers of being alone with the opposite sex, or why we should not dress immodestly, or the dangers of alcohol. There are no absolutes anymore; sin is no longer "*exceedingly sinful.*" We have become what the prior generation preached against; we have become lukewarm Laodiceans!

The Ecumenical Movement has infiltrated the church with false doctrine which will one day lead to a worship of the Antichrist!

3. The final church loses the Scriptures.

Lastly, the final church is identified by losing its hold on the Holy Scriptures, the Word of God. After all the negative things the Lord says in a rebuke to this church of the Laodiceans, look what He counsels them to do:

Revelation 3:18 *"I counsel thee to buy of me gold tried in the fire, that thou mayest be rich; and white raiment, that thou mayest be clothed, and that the shame of thy nakedness do not appear; and anoint thine eyes with eyesalve, that thou mayest see."*

What is this "gold" they are advised to buy, and where do they purchase it? It cannot be literal gold, for they use that for mere street pavement in Heaven. So, what is this "gold" that the final end-times church of the Laodiceans needs so desperately? Think about it, what is more valuable than all the wealth in the world? What is the one thing that the Lord says is more valuable than even His name?

Psalm 138:2 *"I will worship toward thy holy temple, and praise thy name for thy lovingkindness and for thy truth: for thou hast magnified thy word above all thy name."*

The Final Church of the End-times Loses the Word of God.

Just prior to the rapture, the final church has lost its identity; it takes no stand on moral issues, and ultimately has lost its hold on the Bible. The Lord told them to buy gold because they lost theirs, *that gold is the Word of God.*

The church needs to get back to the gold standard.

One of the main responsibilities of the Church is to uphold and defend the Word of God.

1Timothy 3:15 *But if I tarry long, that thou mayest know how thou oughtest to behave thyself in the house of God, which is the church of the living God, the pillar and ground of the truth.*

The Church is not the truth; the Church is the protector and promotor of the truth, which is the Word of God.

The Catholic Church believes the Pope is the authority, which is why they declared it illegal to print the Scriptures in English. This has caused the death of countless thousands of martyrs throughout history. True Bible believers know that the church is not the final authority on matters of faith and practice; the Word of God is the final authority. The church is to preach, print, protect, guard, promote, and defend the Word of God.

With that made clear, now we must discern what exactly is the Word of God.

The Word of God is what God Has Said

Genesis 3:1-3 *"Now the serpent was more subtil than any beast of the field which the LORD God had made. And he said unto the woman, Yea, hath God said, Ye shall not eat of every tree of the garden? And the woman said unto the serpent, We may eat of the fruit of the trees of the garden: But of the fruit of the tree which is in the midst of the garden, God hath said, Ye shall not eat of it, neither shall ye touch it, lest ye die.*

In the text, both Satan and Eve understood that the Word of God consisted of what God had said to man. It really is that simple; the Word of God is "what God said." When we teach or preach to others, we need to make it clear that we are not giving our opinion about things but relaying to them what God has said in His Word.

First usage of the term "WORD OF GOD"

1 Samuel 9:27 *And as they were going down to the end of the city, Samuel said to Saul, Bid the servant pass on before us, (and he passed on,) but stand thou still a while, that I may shew thee the word of God.*

This is the first time that the phrase "Word of God" is used in your Bible. This makes it very important in relation to the law of first mention, as it sets a precedence. Look back just a little to verse 15 where God first spoke His word to Samuel the day before.

1 Samuel 9:15 *Now the LORD had told Samuel in his ear a day before Saul came, saying,*

Notice that in verse 27 it is STILL the Word of God 24 hours later when quoted by Samuel to Saul. It may or may not have been written down, but it was still the inspired Word of God to man and was to be believed and obeyed.

The Word of God is what
God hath said to man.

What God has said is just as powerful and just as true even when preached, spoken, or read a whole day, a month, or even 6,000 years later. Let's go a little further:

What is Scripture?

The word "Script" is the root word of the word "Scripture." Scripture is God's Word in written form. It is just as much the inspired, perfect Word of God as when it was spoken from God's mouth. Copy those words over a thousand times and it is still God's Word. In fact, Scripture is what Paul said was given by inspiration of God in 2 Timothy 3:16.

Scripture Is What God Has Said in Written Form.

Scripture is synonymous with the Word of God. Scripture and the Word of God are one and the same. Note the following verses:

John 5:38-39 *"And ye have not his word abiding in you: for whom he hath sent, him ye believe not. Search the scriptures; for in them ye think ye have eternal life: and they are they which testify of me."*

John 10:35 *"If he called them gods, unto whom the word of God came, and the scripture cannot be broken;"*

Acts 17:11 *"These were more noble than those in Thessalonica, in that they received the word with all readiness of mind, and searched the scriptures daily, whether those things were so."*

There can be no doubt; the Word of God is synonymous with Scripture. The first usage of the word "Scripture" in the Bible is found in the book of Daniel.

Daniel 10:21 *"But I will shew thee that which is noted in the scripture of truth: and there is none that holdeth with me in these things, but Michael your prince."*

Note carefully how God defines His words within the text itself. You will find this all through the Bible. The Scripture is truth. Truth is the Word of God. Jesus is The Truth!

Scripture and the Word of God are one and the same.

When Scripture is referenced by someone within the Bible, it is always speaking of a copy not an original. Don't be fooled by Greek scholars into thinking only the originals are the perfect inspired Scriptures! Consider the following:

2 Timothy 1:5 *"And that from a child thou hast known the holy scriptures, which are able to make thee wise unto salvation through faith which is in Christ Jesus."*

2 Timothy 3:15 *"When I call to remembrance the unfeigned faith that is in thee, which dwelt first in thy grandmother Lois, and thy mother Eunice; and I am persuaded that in thee also."*

There are no originals nor were there any originals in existence in Paul's day. Do you really think Timothy's mother and grandmother had originals? Do you suppose they had the "originals" hidden under their bed?

Whatever they had were copies, not originals hand-written by Moses. Even the Scriptures at the temple were copies. The originals would have been thousands of years old, written on animal skins. They would have turned to dust by that time. The point I am making here is that Paul referred to these copies as "*holy scriptures*."

The Apostle Paul believed that God's inspired words had been kept from generation to generation through copies and translations.

Friend, you either have to believe this, or you have to believe that Lois and Eunice had the originals written by Moses on lamb skins hidden under their bed!

1 Thessalonians 2:13 *"For this cause also thank we God without ceasing, because, when ye received the word of God*

which ye heard of us, ye received it not as the word of men, but as it is in truth, the word of God, which effectually worketh also in you that believe."

I am very thankful I have the perfect inspired and preserved Word of God I can hold in my hand!

The Word of God is:

PURE: Proverbs 30:5 *"Every word of God is pure: he is a shield unto them that put their trust in him."*

Psalms 19:8 *"The statutes of the LORD are right, rejoicing the heart: the commandment of the LORD is pure, enlightening the eyes."*

PRECIOUS: Psalms 126:6 *"He that goeth forth and weepeth, bearing precious seed, shall doubtless come again with rejoicing, bringing his sheaves with him."*

SETTLED: Psalms 119:89 *"For ever, O LORD, thy word is settled in heaven."*

TRUTH: John 17:17 *"Sanctify them through thy truth: thy word is truth."*
Psalms 119:160 *"Thy word is true from the beginning: and every one of thy righteous judgments endureth for ever."*

POWERFUL: Hebrews 4:*12 "For the word of God is quick, and powerful, and sharper than any twoedged sword, piercing even to the dividing asunder of soul and spirit, and of the joints and marrow, and is a discerner of the thoughts and intents of the heart."*

INSPIRED: 2 Timothy 3:16 *"All scripture is given by inspiration of God, and is profitable for doctrine, for reproof, for correction, for instruction in righteousness:"*

PRESERVED: Psalms 12:6-7 *"The words of the LORD are pure words: as silver tried in a furnace of earth, purified seven times. Thou shalt keep them, O LORD, thou shalt preserve them from this generation for ever."*

ETERNAL: Psalms 119:160 *"Thy word is true from the beginning: and every one of thy righteous judgments endureth forever."*

John 1:1 *"In the beginning was the Word, and the Word was with God, and the Word was God."*

PERFECT: Psalms 19:7 *"The law of the LORD is perfect, converting the soul: the testimony of the LORD is sure, making wise the simple."*

Psalms 118:9 *"It is better to trust in the LORD than to put confidence in princes."*

Psalm 118:9 is the middle verse of the King James Bible. ***The Lord*** is at the very center of our Bible.

Where is the Word of God today?

If I ask ten different people at a church on Sunday morning where the Word of God is today, I would get several different answers. Before you read any further, would you pause for a moment and consider that question? What have you decided is the perfect, inspired Word of God?

Before we discuss where the Word of God is today, we need to learn where it was during the preceding Church Age. Since our generation loses it, we need to go back to the last generation and see what they believed was the Word of God.

The Church Age that existed right before the Church of the Laodiceans was the church in Philadelphia.

In Revelation, Jesus complimented the Philadelphia church for their attitude towards His Word. He bragged that they had "*kept*" His word and He gave them an open door.

Revelation 3:7-8 *"And to the angel of the church in Philadelphia write; These things saith he that is holy, he that is true, he that hath the key of David, he that openeth, and no man shutteth; and shutteth, and no man openeth; I know thy works: behold, I have set before thee an open door, and no man can shut it: for thou hast a little strength, and* ***hast kept my word****, and hast not denied my name."*

The church in Philadelphia covers the years 1700-1901, with its meaning defined as 'brotherly love.' Before I reveal what they considered the Word of God, I want to give you just a brief description of what they did with the Word of God.

The Philadelphia church was a time of great revivals as well as two *great awakenings*. God raised up great men like George Whitefield, who could be heard a mile away without a microphone in the 1730's. He once said he could tell when men were under conviction as he preached when he could see the streaks on their coal stained faces from the tears. Jonathan Edwards preached the famous sermon, "*Sinners in the Hands of an Angry God*," where he gave the illustration of a spider hanging over hell by a web.

Men grabbed the pillars of the sanctuary crying out in fear that they too were going to fall into hell!

God raised up John and Charles Wesley, Charles Spurgeon and D. L. Moody who shook entire continents for God in the 1800's! America took its place as the Christian nation of the world during this time, but what was the Bible they considered to be the Word of God during this amazing generation?

An Open Door

The last Church Age was blessed with an open door because they kept His Word. I dare say 99 percent of the folks reading this book have never experienced a great moving of God in their life or a church-wide revival. I am not talking about a guest speaker who made you laugh and feel good, or a nationally-acclaimed gospel singer coming and packing out a stadium and stirring your emotions with his music. I am talking about the moving of the Holy Ghost of God and Him bringing men and women under great conviction! I don't mean a laughing revival. I mean a moving of God where men and women get on their faces before God in a spirit of great sorrow and repentance! I am talking about people weeping over sins and praying for hours, confessing, seeking forgiveness from others, and turning their community upside down for the Lord. My dear friends, you and I can only read about such things because they happened to the prior generation of churches.

What has changed in our day? Could it be we have lost the Word of God?

What was the Bible they considered to be the Holy Scriptures in D.L. Moody's day when he shook two continents for God? What was the book that Whitefield and Edwards preached from? What was the Bible that brought about the two *great awakenings*?

Which Bible caused grown men to weep with great conviction?

They asked John Wesley one day "Why do the multitudes come out in the fields to hear you?" He replied, "I don't know, I just set myself on fire and the people come to watch me burn."

What Bible caused people to stand in the rain to hear John Wesley as he "lit himself on fire?" Was it the *originals* we hear so much about today, or did he preach from the *Greek and Hebrew*? I can tell you most assuredly, it was none of those. Did he preach from the NIV or the ESV? That is impossible, because those translations of the Bible were written during the Laodicean Age, after the year 1901. Wouldn't you like to have the book of God that those men trusted in? What Bible was used during the greatest Church Age of all? What is the GOLD that Jesus said we need and where do we buy it?

The answer: The King James Bible printed in 1611
The Bible used by all English-speaking people during the greatest Church Age of all time was none other than the **King James Bible of 1611**. Without getting into the history of English translations up through the 1500's, I can tell you with all certainty that the King James Bible was the only English Bible used from the years 1700-1901. This is an undisputed fact and is not questioned by anyone who has studied church history.

The King James Bible was the only English Bible used until 1901.

The statements I just made about the last church age under the King James Bible cannot be refuted. It is just shocking to hear folks today criticize the King James Bible. If you choose to use a more modern version, that is one thing, but why would anyone scoff at the Bible that reached more souls than any other Bible in history? Rather, I would think we might want to go examine it and see why it shook the world. **Better yet, let's trade in the Bible that is not working for the old King James!**

How are our Churches doing since 1901 with the dozens of new translations?

I have spoken in churches where the congregation uses several different modern versions of the Bible; each one is different. Some versions have whole verses missing from the text and words changed. Many of the modern versions have changed "virgin" to maid. This brings confusion into the church and "*God is not the author of confusion.*" (I Corinthians 14:33) Maybe we need to return to the tried and proven Word of God that our forefathers used, the King James Bible. Have you ever wondered why we traded in the old for the new?

Please Pardon my Boldness

I know great men of God that use modern translations. I have preacher friends in the ministry that I love and respect that use other versions of the Bible. I still love them, and God is using them. I am not here to bash or belittle anyone. I have travailed and wept over this chapter! I would not hurt my fellow preachers and friends for anything in the world, but my brethren, *we are losing the Word of God in our generation!* Because of that, we are losing the power of God and the open door that we so desperately need. We have the same God that Moody and Whitefield had, but churches of today are not seeing the results that they once did. What has changed? Has God changed? Has man changed?

Only one thing has changed - the Word of God that we read, study, and teach.

I could share many of the issues I have with modern translations, but I chose instead to passionately share the great majesty and influence that the King James Bible had on the world during the prior Church Age. If that does not move you to at least research and pray about this issue, nothing more I say will matter. We will be friends and agree to disagree.

The Word of God for me

I cannot decide the Word of God for you today. That is something you must decide for yourself. I have very passionately tried to show you how the Lord used the King James Bible to reach the world.

From 1650-1950, no one questioned the perfection and superiority of the King James Bible.

I made my decision about the Word of God just a few months after I got saved in 1981. I did not understand these things I just shared with you in this chapter. I was a brand-new Christian, just 21 years of age and in the last year of my Naval enlistment. I got born again while home on leave. I returned to the ship with *The Living Bible* translation in my sea bag. I still remember the green cover it had and the gold lettering.

It was my first Bible and I was very thankful for it. I am still thankful for it; the Lord used that Bible in my life for a short time. A few weeks later, my sister Julie sent me a brand-new leather-bound *King James Bible*! I will never forget what it was like reading that blessed book for the first time. I had no knowledge of the controversy surrounding modern translations; all I knew was MY HEART BURNED when I read that one. I was like David of old when he picked up the sword of Goliath and exclaimed, "*There's none like that one*." I have never used a modern version since that day in 1981. Years later, after more than 1,000 hours of study about the Word of God, it became a conviction instead of a preference. NOTE: I have written a book called *HATH GOD SAID* that is available on Amazon Kindle. It is also in PDF on my website.

The King James Bible is the perfect and preserved Word of God!

If I did not believe the King James Bible was the perfect and preserved Word of God, I would put it away and begin my search for the true Word of God

.

If you have studied this issue and have come to another conclusion, I am not upset with you. My conviction may not be your conviction. I have shared my soul with you in this chapter. I have passionately tried to convey to you what the Lord laid on my heart concerning how the church in the last generation loses the Word of God. If you do not see it my way and decide the Word of God is better preserved in a modern translation, I can only request that you sincerely consider these things that I have shared with you.

Psalms 12:6-7 *"The words of the LORD are pure words: as silver tried in a furnace of earth, purified seven times. Thou shalt* ***keep*** *them, O LORD, thou shalt* ***preserve*** *them from this generation* ***forever****."*

Somewhere in the world God has preserved His Word. I believe the last generation had the perfect Word of God and knew they did. They did not doubt it nor try to improve it. They believed it for what it was, the perfect and preserved Word of God, the King James Bible. They evangelized the world with it for 300 years.

Our generation has dozens of modern versions, many of them did not last for more than a few years. I would challenge you to do a study of the men behind the new versions. I believe you would be shocked to find out the names and doctrinal positions of many of these men. I doubt anyone shed their blood, were tortured or suffered financial ruin over a modern version.

Just look at the confused mess we are in today! I have decided where the Word of God is in my life; I hope that if you have not yet decided, that something I have said will influence your choice. The Lord counsels us to "*buy of me gold tried in the fire*." I say the church needs to consider getting back on the "gold standard."

Many translations contain the Word of God.
The King James Bible IS the Word of God!

Satan's Grand Deception

Genesis 3:1 *"Now the serpent was more subtil than any beast of the field which the LORD God had made. And he said unto the woman, Yea, hath God said, Ye shall not eat of every tree of the garden?"*

The Devil starts out positive here: "*Yea hath God said?*" The Word of God is what God has said. The Devil *knows* that to be true even though many today do not. I want to show you something in this passage. "*Yea, hath God said, Ye shall not eat of every tree of the garden?*" Satan is not asking a question; he is making a rhetorical statement. He is planting seeds of doubt in Eve's mind. Satan already knows the answer.

In Genesis 3:2-3 we read, "*And the woman said unto the*

serpent, We may eat of the fruit of the trees of the garden. But of the fruit of the tree which is in the midst of the garden, God hath said, Ye shall not eat of it, neither shall ye touch it, lest ye die."

The first thing we learn way back in Genesis 3:1, is that Satan is very subtle. He is very "crafty" about his business of deceiving. I want you to notice that Satan got Eve to question the validity of the Word of God. Satan told Eve what God had told Adam. "*Yea, hath God said, Ye shall not eat of every tree of the garden?*" Satan was quoting the Word of God in a demeaning way. Eve answers and says, "*God hath said, Ye shall not eat of it, neither shall ye touch it lest ye die.*" Eve is quoting what God had said to her husband, Adam. That's right; Eve was not there when God told Adam not to eat of this fruit.

Eve got the Word of God
from Adam second-hand!

The battle has always been over "*Hath God said*?" Eve got the Word of God from Adam, a second-hand telling of what God had told him. The serpent got Eve to question this second-hand Word of God. Once he got her to question the accuracy of those words, it was easy to get her to doubt the validity of those words.

Since she did not hear God say it; how could she know Adam translated it accurately?

Do you see the point I am trying to make?

The Word of God has been revealed to all of us second-hand. There can be no doubt that it has come to everyone second-hand for the last 2,000 years, yet it is still the perfect and preserved Word of God. Very few in history have ever gotten the Word of God first-hand. Adam heard the voice of God; Moses did, too. A few of the prophets received it first-hand, but 99.999 percent of the world has gotten the Word of God SECOND-HAND! Have you ever stopped to think about this?

Preachers are always talking about the *originals*. Theologians are always referring to the *original manuscripts*. Somehow the *originals* sound more legitimate. The thought of old original manuscripts written by the Apostle Paul gives you the feeling they are more accurate than a copy, but don't you believe it! That is the exact line that Satan used way back in the garden! There are no originals anywhere on planet earth. Even the Dead Sea Scrolls are not *originals* penned by Moses' own hand.

Skeptical?

Some of you do not believe me, do you? You have heard about originals all your life and have never had anyone challenge you. I have studied this issue over 1,000 hours and I assure you – there are no originals anywhere on planet earth. There were no originals when Jesus walked the earth 2,000 years ago! I challenge you to do some study and direct me to an original manuscript, and prove me wrong! Friends, we have been deceived and it has caused many to begin to doubt the perfection of their English Bible that turned the world upside down for 300 years.

"Hath God Said?"

Today, Satan is still getting man to question the second-hand Word of God by deceiving good men into thinking the perfect Word of God can only be found in the originals by way of Greek and Hebrew manuscripts. These theologians, these men with doctorate degrees who stand before us, are often good and sincere men who honestly believe they are doing God service.

These men who try to get you to trust in the so called "originals" are doing the same thing Satan did to Eve! Don't fall for it!

The Battle over God's Words

The battle has always been over the Bible. Man started out his days nearly six thousand years ago questioning the Word of God, and it appears he will end his days with the same demise and confusion. The martyrs of old were all persecuted over one main issue: THE WORD OF GOD! From the popes of Rome to the kings and queens of England, the persecutions have arisen over whether the "Church" or the "Bible" is the ultimate authority. The Pope had decreed it was unlawful to translate the Latin Bible into English, the language of the common man. This kept the people at the mercy of the clergy to know the truth. William Tyndale said the following to a Catholic Bishop in the early 1500's:

"I defy the Pope and all his laws. If God spare my life, ere many years, I will cause a boy who drives the plough to know more of the Scriptures than you do."

William Tyndale followed through with that vow when in 1526, he published the Scriptures in English. He was burned at the stake in 1536. His last words were: "Oh God open the eyes of the King of England." That prayer was answered in 1604 with the authorization from King James to begin the translation work for the 1611 King James Bible.

The enemy of the Word of God throughout history has always been religious institutions! The battle is the same today that was fought by our forefathers. The difference today is many have neither the discernment nor the backbone to stand "*...for the faith which was once delivered unto the saints.*"

Joshua 24:15 "*...choose you this day whom ye will serve...*"

Here are your choices for the Word of God today.

1. Modern translation of your choosing.

There have been several modern translations produced since 1901. Most of them are seldom used today. The NIV, the ESV, and the NKJV are the most popular today. Keep in mind these translations differ from the King James as well as each other, resulting in much confusion.

2. The Original Autographs. The 'Original' as referring to the hand-written parchments by Moses, Paul, etc. This is really not an option, because these do not exist anywhere on planet earth. I included them in the list because of the misconception that so many have today about original scripts. I *double-dog dare you* to prove me wrong on this point!

3. Hebrew and Greek Texts. I will not discuss the Hebrew Texts, but there are several points I want to make about Biblical Greek texts:

- Nobody speaks Koine Greek today.
-There are many definitions for each Greek word.
-How can you know which Greek text is right?
-Many of the Greek definitions are in error.
-There are several Greek texts... all differ from each other.

History of the Greek

The Greek Text was almost lost to the world until a Scholar named **Erasmus** who hated the Catholic Latin Vulgate Bible, began his work of finding and restoring the Greek Manuscripts. Erasmus Produced a Greek text in 1516 that sparked the Reformation. He revised it again in 1519, 1522, 1527, and 1535. Erasmus' Greek went through even more transformations later. **Robert Stephanus** published four editions from 1546-1551. **Theodore Beza** (Beza Greek text) published several editions from 1565-1598. It is Beza's 1598 edition and Stephanus' 1550-1551 editions of Greek that the King James translators had in 1604.

Stephanus followed the Erasmus Greek closely in his work. From 1624-1641 the **Elzevir brothers** published 3 editions of Greek.

The point is, there are many editions of Greek Text and they are all different. There was no perfect Greek Text in 1604, and there is no perfect Greek Text today.

4. The King James Bible printed in 1611.

The Bible I refer to as GOLD, was translated by fifty-four of the greatest scholars ever assembled in the history of the world. These fifty-four men could converse in Greek like no one can today. One of the translators, *Lancelot Andrews*, could speak 21 languages. It was a joke amongst them that he could have interpreted for everyone at the Tower of Babel. Another translator, *Miles Smith*, who wrote the preface to the King James Bible called 'The Translators to the Reader,' was nicknamed, "A Walking Library." Each man on the translating committee had veto power over every word in the translation. There was no "majority rule" as is the case of *all* the modern translations.

The King James Bible was all preachers had for over 300 years before the new versions came on the scene. I have given you these options to consider. Please make it a matter of prayer before you decide what Bible is to be the final authority in your life.

The Church of the Laodiceans is not just a symptom of a problem, but a sign of the end of an age - the Church Age.

Illustrated by my sister, Deb Porter

The world ends right where it began 6,000 years ago with: a bride, some liberating fruit, and a serpent.

Isaiah 46:10a *"Declaring the end from the beginning, and from ancient times the things that are not yet done..."*

Do you want to know how it all ends? Go back to the beginning. It all ends just like it began 6,000 years ago with a bride named Eve-- being wooed by a serpent with fruit that liberates the soul.

Laodiceans is defined as "the rights of the people." We have the last church filled with people wanting their way, wanting their rights, being wooed by Satan into believing the King James Bible is an old-fashioned, out-of-date book that is filled with legalistic views that no longer apply today. Satan offers the great-tasting fruit of modern watered-down versions that liberate and make us feel better about ourselves. Don't be fooled by Satan's lies.

The Ticking Nuclear Clock

War broke out on the earth as soon as Adam took the first bite of the forbidden fruit.

The first deadly weapon was a simple rock in the hand of Cain as he took the life of his own brother. Since that time the weapons of war have increased: in number, in violence, and in effect. The final war upon the earth is going to be cataclysmic! It is described in the Scriptures as so horrific that if God doesn't intervene, the entire world will perish.

Mark 13:20 *"And except that the Lord had shortened those days, no flesh should be saved..."*

It is very plain in Scripture that the final generation upon the earth before the Lord returns has the potential to destroy all of mankind. I believe that day is here, and it is only by the grace of God we have not already done so. For this reason, I believe nuclear war is a ticking clock that is mere minutes away from striking midnight.

Wars and Rumors of Wars

The study of history is the study of war. We began with a war against God in the Garden of Eden, and we will end with a final war against Christ at Armageddon. You will have a hard time looking back in history to find a time of world peace. It seems like war is in our nature and we simply must have it.

"In case of rain, the war will be held in the auditorium"

Prussian Proverb

Historical artifacts, art, and civilizations are dated by wars. For instance, there are pre-war era guitars, Civil War era banjos, and Revolutionary era furniture. Jesus spoke of "*wars and rumors of wars*" as if to confirm that every generation and people would be affected by war.

The Final Generation

For the first time ever, in our generation the world has the capability to destroy itself. Never in prior history has that been possible. When George Washington read the following passage in 1776, do you suppose it made much sense to him as he looked at his flintlock rifle?

Matthew 24:21-22 *"For then shall be great tribulation, such as was not since the beginning of the world to this time, no, nor ever shall be. And except those days should be shortened, there should no flesh be saved: but for the elect's sake those days shall be shortened."*

History of Warfare

For about 5,000 years of human history, very little changed concerning warfare. Swords, spears, bows and clubs were the weaponry to choose from. It was approximately 1000 A.D. when gunpowder was first used in warfare. This changed how man would practice war. Portable cannons were first used in 1450 A.D. by the French who also invented the flintlock rifle in early 1600. In the 1850's the breach loading rifle was introduced. In the early 1900's the machine gun was first used in warfare. In 1905, the Germans invented the first submarine called a U-boat. In 1915 just a few years after the Wright Brothers, the Germans introduced the first fighter planes with workable machine guns. After 5,900 years of human history, warfare had evolved from the primitive swords and spears to firing projectiles from airplanes and submersible boats. But the world had not seen anything yet! Man was just getting started in his quest to wage war and annihilate cities and kingdoms.

Nuclear Age

The **Atomic Age***, also known as the* **Atomic** *Era, is the period of history following the detonation of the first nuclear ("***atomic***") bomb, on July 16, 1945 during World War II.* Wikipedia

In the late 1930's the race was on between Germany and the

United States to be the first to build a nuclear bomb. On June 7, 1942, a physicist named J. Robert Oppenheimer was appointed director of the highly secretive *Manhattan Project* to develop a nuclear weapon for the United States.

The Manhattan Project
From ushistory.org

Early in 1939, the world's scientific community discovered that German physicists had learned the secrets of splitting a uranium atom. Fears soon spread over the possibility of Nazi scientists utilizing that energy to produce a bomb capable of unspeakable destruction.

Scientists **ALBERT EINSTEIN**, who fled Nazi persecution, and **ENRICO FERMI**, who escaped Fascist Italy, were now living in the United States. They agreed that the President must be informed of the dangers of atomic technology in the hands of the Axis powers. Fermi traveled to Washington in March to express his concerns to government officials. But few shared his uneasiness.

Einstein penned a letter to President Roosevelt urging the development of an atomic research program later that year. Roosevelt saw neither the necessity nor the utility for such a project but agreed to proceed slowly. In late 1941, the American effort to design and build an **ATOMIC BOMB** received its code name — the **MANHATTAN PROJECT**.

At first the research was based at only a few universities — Columbia University, the University of Chicago and the University of California at Berkeley. A breakthrough occurred in December 1942 when Fermi led a group of physicists to produce the first controlled **NUCLEAR CHAIN REACTION** under the grandstands of **STAGG FIELD** at the University of Chicago.

After this milestone, funds were allocated more freely, and the project advanced at breakneck speed. Nuclear facilities were built at Oak Ridge, Tennessee and Hanford, Washington. The main assembly plant was built at **LOS ALAMOS, NEW MEXICO**. **ROBERT OPPENHEIMER** was put in charge of putting the pieces together at Los Alamos. After the final bill was tallied, nearly $2 billion had been spent on research and development of the atomic bomb. The Manhattan Project employed over 120,000 Americans.

Secrecy was paramount. Neither the Germans nor the Japanese could learn of the project. Roosevelt and Churchill also agreed that Stalin would be kept in the dark. Consequently, there was no public awareness or debate. Keeping 120,000 people quiet would be impossible; therefore, only a small privileged cadre of inner scientists and officials knew about the atomic bomb's development. In fact, Vice-President Truman had never heard of the Manhattan Project until he became President Truman.

Although the Axis powers remained unaware of the efforts at Los Alamos, American leaders later learned that a Soviet spy named **KLAUS FUCHS** had penetrated the inner circle of scientists.

By the summer of 1945, Oppenheimer was ready to test the first bomb. On July 16, 1945, at **TRINITY SITE** near **ALAMOGORDO, NEW MEXICO**, scientists of the Manhattan Project readied themselves to watch the detonation of the world's first atomic bomb. The device was affixed to a 100-foot tower and discharged just before dawn. No one was properly prepared for the result.

A blinding flash visible for 200 miles lit up the morning sky. A mushroom cloud reached 40,000 feet, blowing out windows of civilian homes up to 100 miles away. When the cloud returned to earth it created a half-mile wide crater metamorphosing sand into glass. A bogus cover-up story was quickly released, explaining that a huge ammunition dump had just exploded in the desert. Soon word reached President Truman in Potsdam, Germany that the project was successful.

The world had entered the nuclear age.

AUTHOR	ushistory.org
TITLE OF PAGE	The Manhattan Project
TITLE OF PROGRAM	*U.S. History Online Textbook*
URL OF PAGE	http://www.ushistory.org/us/51f.asp
DATE OF ACCESS	Thursday, September 13, 2018
COPYRIGHT	2018

If the nuclear bomb was not bad enough, the hydrogen bomb was introduced in 1952. It was successfully tested by the United States in the Marshall Islands. It is 1,000 times more powerful than the bombs dropped on Japan. Can you imagine the destructive force of just one of these going off in a major city? The death toll would be in the millions!

I am trying to get you to see that warfare was taken to an all new level during the Nuclear Age. I find it interesting that the nuclear age began shortly before the rebirth of the nation of Israel. The hydrogen bomb has existed for almost 70 years. What type of warfare do you suppose has been invented that we do not know about?

Let us fast forward our study to modern times.

Intercontinental Ballistic Missile (ICBM)

These are current day missiles that can be armed with nuclear warheads and can reach targets over 3,000 miles away. It is common knowledge that Russia has thousands of ICBM's aimed at America right now. Each one would make the bombs dropped on Japan in 1945 look like firecrackers in comparison. Can you comprehend that?

I have read that America has weapons that have not even been tested because we are not sure what they will do -- and I believe it is true. Though nobody can be sure, it is believed there are about 15,000 nuclear warheads in the world controlled by nine countries. These countries are USA, Russia, the UK, France, India, Pakistan, North Korea, China and Israel. It is just a matter of time before tragedy strikes. It is possible that Israel could be annihilated in a moment even though we know from the Bible that will not happen. This leads me to believe the rapture is soon. Israel has more enemies today than ever before, yet her security seems assured.

World Kingdoms are in Place

The end-time world kingdoms are all in place and ready to fulfill Bible prophecy. Russia, Iran, China, Syria, and of course Israel, are all in their place. It appears that Russia and China are already practicing for their role in the last days as you can read in the following article:

AFP•September 11, 2018

Chita (Russia) (AFP) - Russia launched Tuesday what it called its largest ever military drills, with hundreds of thousands of troops taking part along with Chinese soldiers in a show of force NATO condemned as a rehearsal for "large-scale conflict."

President Vladimir Putin is expected to attend the games after hosting an economic forum in Russia's far eastern city Vladivostok where his Chinese counterpart Xi Jinping is one of the prominent guests.

The week-long war games dubbed "Vostok-2018"(East-2018) "have kicked off" in far eastern Russia, the defence ministry said.

Taking part in the drills are around 300,000 soldiers, 36,000 military vehicles, 80 ships and 1,000 aircraft, helicopters and drones.

Some 3,500 Chinese troops will take part in the exercise.

Putin praised Russia's increasingly close ties with China as he met Xi at the economic forum in Vladivostok on Tuesday.

"We have trustworthy ties in political, security and defence spheres," the Russian leader said.

Xi for his part said the two countries' "friendship is getting stronger all the time."

The drills, which also include Mongolian soldiers, have been condemned by NATO as a rehearsal for "large-scale conflict". The military exercises come at a time of escalating tensions between Moscow and the West over accusations of Russian interference in western affairs and conflicts in Ukraine and Syria.

The Russian army has compared the show of force to the USSR's 1981 war games that saw between 100,000 and 150,000 Warsaw Pact soldiers take part in "Zapad-81" (West-81) -- the largest military exercises of the Soviet era.

"Imagine 36,000 military vehicles moving at the same time: tanks, armoured personnel carriers, infantry fighting vehicles -- and all of this, of course, in conditions as close to a combat situation as possible,"

Shoigu said.

The exercises will be held across nine training ranges and three seas: the Sea of Japan, the Bering Sea and the Sea of Okhotsk.

NATO said that Vostok-2018 "demonstrates Russia's focus on exercising large-scale conflict".

Putin's spokesman Dmitry Peskov dismissed western concerns on Tuesday. "These are very important drills but they are part of routine annual work to develop the armed forces," he told journalists.

Relations between Russia and the West declined sharply in 2014 with Moscow's annexation of Crimea and the outbreak of a Kremlin-backed uprising in eastern Ukraine.

Russia's previous military exercise in the region, Vostok-2014, was almost half the size, with 155,000 soldiers participating.

The country's war games in Eastern Europe last year, Zapad-2017, saw 12,700 troops take part, according to Moscow. Ukraine and the Baltic states said the true number was far bigger.
Maxime POPOV
AFP • September 11, 2018

The following article is from *the Sun News* dated September 12, 2018. I included just a portion which further describes the same exercise between Russia and China.

The Vostok 2018 drills - taking place in eastern Siberia close to the border with China - involve 300,000 Russian troops as well as joint exercises with the Chinese army.
"This is the first time our army and fleet have undergone such a difficult and large-scale test," said President Putin.

The exercises, that involve over a thousand military aircraft as well as up to 36,000 tanks, come amid tense relations between Russia and the West that have fallen to a post-Cold War low.

The Chinese media have described the People's Liberation Army involvement in the drills as the country's largest-ever dispatch of forces abroad for war games.

The Russian Army has compared the show of force to the USSR's 1981 Zapad war games that saw around 150,000 Warsaw Pact soldiers take part in the largest military exercises of the Soviet era.

Yet the drills - to take place across several training grounds - will dwarf even this notorious exercise when it comes to scale.

Military leaders released video footage of military vehicles, planes, helicopters and ships getting into position for the initial stage of the drills.

The jaw-dropping numbers involved in the Vostok-2018 include:

- Around 300,000 battle-ready Russian troops
- More than 1,000 planes, helicopters, and drones.
- 36,000 tanks and armoured personal carriers.
- More than 80 ships and naval support vessels.
- An estimated 30 aircraft from the Chinese air force.
- Mongolian troops will also join the battles.
- Russia has one million military personnel in total.

The Sun/UK News Sept 13, 2018
www.thesun.co.uk/news/7248874/v/

Those are some shocking statistics about how big these wargames were. War is serious business and it appears we are getting very close to a major and final one.

What does it all mean?

Please do not mistake my rhetoric and sarcasm about *war* for my being anti-war. God led Israel into battle on many occasions. Revelation 19:11 speaking of Jesus says: *"...in righteousness he doth judge and make war.*" Solomon said it this way in Ecclesiastes 3:8: "*A time to love, and a time to hate; a time of war, and a time of peace.*"

If you read carefully the article I cited about *The Manhattan Project*, then you should grasp the necessity of war. Had America not built the Atom bomb, Germany would have done so and most likely would have won the war and taken over the entire world. Many historians believe that the Atom bombs dropped on Japan saved lives by ending the war early. The point of all this is to get you to see the lateness of the hour. Since 1945, man has grown both in technology and in his ability to wage war.

It all boils down to this: We are at five minutes to midnight on the nuclear clock!

God's Line in the Sand

Since man has opened the door to the nuclear age, it seems like we've crossed a line that God has drawn in the sand. God has some eternal boundaries that He will not allow man to cross. This is a little 'deep' so read carefully as I share some eternal boundaries or lines in the sand that God will not allow man to cross.

1. God had a line in the sand in Genesis 3 that Adam was not to cross. Look what the Lord said about the results of Adam's disobedience:

Genesis 3:22-23 "*And the LORD God said, Behold, the man is become as one of us, to know good and evil: and now, lest he put forth his hand, and take also of the tree of life, and eat, and live for ever: Therefore the LORD God sent him forth from the garden of Eden, to till the ground from whence he was taken.*"

Have you ever given thought to what the Lord is saying here? There was a line that man could not be allowed to cross. It is possible that Adam would have had access to immortality had God not intervened, but I am not sure. When man crossed that line, God was quite drastic in His response.

2. Another example of man crossing a line in the sand is here:

Genesis 6:5 "*And GOD saw that the wickedness of man was great in the earth, and that every imagination of the thoughts of his heart was only evil continually.*"

This, of course, brought about the flood that killed the entire human race. Only eight souls entered the ark and were saved. Man had crossed a line in the sand and God intervened in a drastic way.

3. Another example is the story of the 'Tower of Babel' here:

Genesis 11:6 "*And the LORD said, Behold, the people is one, and they have all one language; and this they begin to do: and now nothing will be restrained from them, which they have imagined to do.*

Not everyone agrees on what exactly this tower was, but we know this; man was about to cross a line in the sand that would have had eternal consequences. God intervened and stopped it.

I believe we are on the brink of another line in the sand as we progress in the nuclear age. We are meddling with things that are not meant to be meddled with. Things like CERN, a super conductor in Switzerland where scientists are trying to find the "God particle" that holds the atoms together. There are some who fear they are going to open a door or a portal into another dimension. Opening this door may cross a line in the sand that God does not want us to cross. If so, what will God do to intervene this time?

I believe a portal will be opened at the middle of the Tribulation in Revelation 9 when Satan opens the bottomless pit and releases "Hell on earth." It is my personal opinion that God will not allow this line to be crossed before that time.

The nuclear clock is ticking down. We are in the final hours before God ends this age, removes the church, and begins Daniel's 70th week.

Daniel's Ticking Clock

There is a hidden clock ticking within the book of Daniel that many prophecy teachings do not address. This marking of time refers to the existence of historic and end-time kingdoms, or civilizations. They are spoken of clearly in Daniel, Chapters 2 and 7; and in Revelation 13. Upon study, you will find the kingdoms mentioned in these ancient scriptures have been proven true in documented history, which lends credible evidence to the existence of a final kingdom before the second coming of Christ. Remember, God foreknew and foretells this wisdom to those who seek.

Shockingly, the components of this final kingdom are already here! The United Nations, European Union, and World Council of Churches all boldly exist *right now* and will combine under Satan's plan for the *One World Order*. According to Scripture, when the Church is raptured, the Antichrist will soon-after be crowned as head of this world order and will rule all humanity.

Each one-world branch is currently--and anxiously-- awaiting its moment for power and control in the timeline of history. In other words, it is five minutes to midnight on Daniel's ticking clock!

Globalism is here

A one world kingdom would be what leaders call 'globalism.' This term is a household word even now. We hear about global markets, global currency, global trade, and global unity, and of course, global war. The whole world is linked together through the internet, stock market, and banking. It is not difficult to see that this end-time system appears to be in place and ready to go.

The whole world is now ready to embrace globalism.

If you do not believe me, look at the following quotes concerning the subject. If you are at least 50 years of age you should recognize most of these people

.

"Globalization is the central reality of our time. It is coming, and you can't stop it!" Bill Clinton State of the Union Address, January 2000

"If one word encapsulates the changes we are living through, it is globalization. It is the future of the world as we know it."
Former secretary general of the United Nation, Kofi Annan

Back in the year 2000, the prime ministers of Great Britain, the Netherlands, Sweden, and the chancellor of Germany all banded together to collectively write, "We all embrace the potential of globalization. It is the future of the world as we know it." "The New Left Takes on the World" *Washington Post,* September 6, 2000, p. A19

"As the world continues to change and we become more connected to each other, globalization will bring both benefits and disruptions to our lives. But either way, it's here, and it's not going away."~ Barack Obama

"I support freedom and I support a free market economy, but it should be a socially oriented market economy. I support globalization, but it should be globalization with a human face." ~ Mikhail Gorbachev

"The Internet is becoming the town square for the global village of tomorrow." ~ Bill Gates

"Some even believe we (the Rockefeller family) are part of a secret cabal working against the best interests of the United States, characterizing my family and me as 'internationalists' and of conspiring with others around the world to build a more integrated global political and economic structure - one world, if you will. If that's the charge, I stand guilty, and I am proud of it." ~ David Rockefeller

"We cannot leap into world government through one quick step... The precondition for eventual and genuine globalization is progressive regionalization because by that we move toward larger, more stable, more cooperative units." ~ Zbigniew Brzezinski

"If we allow terrorism to undermine our freedom of action, we could reverse at least part of the palpable gains achieved by postwar globalization. It is incumbent upon us not to allow that to happen."
~ Alan Greenspan

"Globalization has altered the dynamics in the White House, as well as between the White House and the Treasury." ~ George W. Bush

It's All About a Kingdom

As I shared in a prior chapter, the Lord gave dominion of the planet to Adam, to have dominion means to have authority. When Adam sinned, he forfeited the title deed of planet earth to Satan who is seeking to bring in a powerful, one world Kingdom. Why one world? So, Satan can easily control it! This one world system will in fact come into fruition after the church is taken out. Let us look at some Scriptures:

Revelation 6:1-2 *"And I saw when the Lamb opened one of the seals, and I heard, as it were the noise of thunder, one of the four beasts saying, Come and see. And I saw, and behold a white horse: and he that sat on him had a bow; and a crown was given unto him: and he went forth conquering, and to conquer."*

2 Thessalonians 2:3-4 *"Let no man deceive you by any means: for that day shall not come, except there come a falling away first, and that man of sin be revealed, the son of perdition; Who opposeth and exalteth himself above all that is called God, or that is worshipped; so that he as God sitteth in the temple of God, shewing himself that he is God."*

Since the very beginning when Adam and Eve lived in the garden, it has been about kingdoms, lands, and properties, and who is going to have rule over them. From neighbors arguing over property lines, ranchers and the range wars of the wild west, to Civil Wars and even world wars, it is all about controlling kingdoms and lands.

Everything is in place, the clock is ticking down

There is a final world war coming called Armageddon. It too, is about property and redemption. Its prophetic outcome will see the return of planet Earth back to its original owner, the Lord Jesus Christ.

Luke 11:2 *"And he said unto them, When ye pray, say, Our Father which art in heaven, Hallowed be thy name. Thy kingdom come. Thy will be done, as in heaven, so in earth."*

God gave the kingdom to Adam, who forfeited it to Satan. Ever since, the kingdoms of the world have been under the dominion of Satan who is working to bring about a one world kingdom. This has been the tough battle that Christians through the ages have been spiritually fighting! That is why Ephesians 6:11 admonishes us to "*Put on the whole armour of God.*" Paul explains why in verse 12:

Ephesians 6:12 *"For we wrestle not against flesh and blood, but against principalities, against powers, against the rulers of the darkness of this world, against spiritual wickedness in high places."*

The Bible states that we don't battle against fellow humans; but against Satan, the grand counterfeiter. He has counterfeit churches, counterfeit Bibles, counterfeit joy and counterfeit love. God is a trinity: Father, Son, and Holy Spirit. Likewise, Satan has a counterfeit trinity: Satan, the Antichrist, and the False Prophet.

All religions will unite

In accordance with Revelation prophecies, current events may point to the possibility of the Pope heading up a one-world church. As evidence of this, please read carefully the article below. It outlines the meeting of Shimon Peres and the Pope in September 2014.

Pay special attention to what I highlighted in the article. This was quite shocking coming from an Israeli, but more importantly, shows just how close we are to the religions of the world all unifying in one religion under the Pope.

Peres, the pope and a plan for world peace

By BRIAN SCHRAUGER
09/09/2014

Two months after completing his term as Israel's ninth president, 91-year-old Shimon Peres was pounding stony pavement at the Vatican. Shimon Peres, a patriarch of today's Israel, wants to leave a legacy. Most in this mode aim for things like monuments, memoirs and money. **Peres's aim is world peace. And in his opinion, Pope Francis, a man he calls "Holy Father," is the one to make it happen.** Vatican spokesmen concur, as does Italy's representative for Islam, who "fully agrees."

On **September 4, 2014**, he was granted an impressive 45-minute meeting with Catholicism's popular pontiff, **a man Peres asserts is more powerful than the United Nations for advocating peace.**

The problem, as Peres sees it, is that "in the past, most wars were motivated by the idea of nationality. Today, however, they are being waged primarily in the name of religion."

In an exclusive interview with the Catholic periodical, Famiglia Cristiana (The Christian Family), Peres divulged his plans: "Perhaps for the first time in history, **the Holy Father is a leader not only respected by many people, but also by different religions and their leaders**."

"In fact," **Peres clarified, "he is perhaps the only truly respected leader" in the world today**.

While Francis has refrained from commenting on Peres's assessment, that same silence permits it. It also permits the framework of Peres's idea to be tested in the crucible of world opinion.

"The United Nations has had its day," Peres opined. "What we need is an organization of United Religions, a United Nations of religions."

"This will be the best way," he continued, "to fight terrorists who kill in the name of faith."

Accordingly, "there should be a Charter of United Religions, just as there is a UN Charter. This is what I have proposed to the pope."

Fulvio Scaglione, deputy managing editor of Famiglia Cristiana, asked, "Would you see the pope as the leader of United Religions?" "Yes," Peres replied. And not only because Francis is a globally respected leader. He is also **the best choice because the world needs "an indisputable moral authority** that says out loud, "No, God does not want this and will not allow it. We must fight against exploitation in the name of God."

Scaglione did not challenge Peres with the question begging to be asked: If abuse of God's name is condemned in God's name, could this not also be, or become, abusive? There is not a public transcript of the meeting between Peres and the pope. But a significant few who are close to Francis had a lot to say about it. All of them were cautious about an institutionalized United Religions organization.

They did not reject it, but they were careful not to endorse it.

The Vatican spokesman for the encounter is Frederico Lombardi, a Jesuit priest. The pope listened to Peres, he said, but "made no personal commitment." He also reminded Peres that the Vatican already has two "suitable" offices for interreligious initiatives.

Andrea Riccardi is founder of Sant'Egidio, an international Catholic lay community committed to ecumenism. He praised Peres for "giving so much weight to the spiritual dimension" in an "encounter with all religions." At the same time, however, Riccardi cautioned against a United Religions organization, calling it "difficult to see an institutionalization of meetings" between religions.

While Catholic spokesmen were cautious about Peres's organizational proposal, they were unambiguous in support of his assessment of their pope. Riccardi agreed that Francis "has very strong moral leadership" that "should continue in service to the unity of the human family."

The Vatican's representative to the United Nations, Archbishop Silvano Maria Tomasi, was effusive about Peres's "perception of Pope Francis, not only as leader of the Catholic Church, but also as a symbol of all religion in the modern world. This is," he said, "a significant turning point in history."

Italy's spokesman for Islam liked everything that Peres said. Handsome, articulate and Western in his manner, Yahya Pallavicini is imam of the al-Wahid Mosque in Milan and vice president of the Islamic Religious Community of Italy, a.k.a. Coreis, a community solicitous toward Christians and Jews.

Pallavicini praised Peres as "a man particularly inspired, combining Jewish faith with political experience. I fully agree" with his proposal to the pope, he said.

In fact, he continued, "Pope Francis may be the most authoritative representative" of "spiritually sensitive" religious leaders in the world today. "I, a Muslim, have much to learn from him," he said.
If one of the Vatican's objectives was to test worldwide reaction to Peres's proposal, response to date indicates mild interest. Outside Italy, mainstream media has barely acknowledged the encounter. Those that have reported it treat it more as a human interest story than hard news.

Here and there voices in pulpits and cyberspace cry danger, but Internet statistics indicate that very few are listening.

If Peres's proposal to the pope gains traction, it will create a global religious union initiated by representatives of the world's three monotheistic religions, a United Religions organization that blends its expression from one-third Judaism, one-third Christianity and one-third Islam. And apparently led from the seven hills of Rome.

The author is the Middle East correspondent and Jerusalem Bureau Chief for IRN-USA Network News. Follow him on Twitter @BrianSchrauger. Originally published at BridgesForPeace.com

Shimon Peres was an Israeli politician who served as the ninth President of Israel, the Prime Minister of Israel, and the Interim Prime Minister, in the 1970s to the 1990s. At the time of his retirement in 2014, he was the world's oldest head of state and was considered the last link to Israel's founding generation. Lived: Aug 02, 1923 - Sep 28, 2016 (age 93) Wikipedia

All governments will unite

Read how the Scripture outlines the crowning of the Antichrist. This happens after the rapture:

Revelation 6:1-2 "[1]And I saw when the Lamb opened one of the seals, and I heard, as it were the noise of thunder, one of the four beasts saying, Come and see. [2]And I saw, and behold a white horse: and he that sat on him had a bow; <u>and a crown was given unto him</u>: and he went forth conquering, and to conquer."

The Antichrist is a leader (currently on the world scene) who will be appointed to rule over *all* countries. The Bible calls those countries the revived Roman Empire. Daniel tells us all about them. Follow along with me:

The Four World Kingdoms: Key Biblical Chapters

Daniel Chapters 2 and 7, and Revelation 13:1-4 all speak of the four kingdoms in history that rule the whole world. Actually, there are five if you count the revived Roman Empire that arises out of the fourth kingdom during the Tribulation.

The four kingdoms came to power from 605 B.C. (Daniel's day) through today, and the fifth will extend to the end of the Tribulation.

There have only been four times in history since the Israelites crossed the Red Sea and left Egypt that the world has been under a one-world dictatorship. These four kingdoms were Babylon, Persia, Greece, and Rome. The fifth one will be during the Tribulation, often called the *revived* Roman Empire simply because it will be a renewal of the fourth empire. It will consist of the ten European nations (as represented by the ten toes and the ten horns mentioned in Daniel).

These nations are in place and even share a common currency. The Antichrist will head up this coming empire. Everything is ready for him to rule the world when the church is gone.

With these thoughts in mind, please read these key passages thoughtfully:

Daniel 2:32-34 *"This image's head was of fine gold, his breast and his arms of silver, his belly and his thighs of brass, His legs of iron, his feet part of iron and part of clay. Thou sawest till that a stone was cut out without hands, which smote the image upon his feet that were of iron and clay, and brake them to pieces."*

Daniel 7:3-7 *"And four great beasts came up from the sea, diverse one from another. The first was like a lion, and had eagle's wings: I beheld till the wings thereof were plucked, and it was lifted up from the earth, and made stand upon the feet as a man, and a man's heart was given to it. And behold another beast, a second, like to a bear, and it raised up itself on one side, and it had three ribs in the mouth of it between the teeth of it: and they said thus unto it, Arise, devour much flesh. After this I beheld, and lo another, like a leopard, which had upon the back of it four wings of a fowl; the beast had also four heads; and dominion was given to it. After this I saw in the night visions, and behold a fourth beast, dreadful and terrible, and strong exceedingly; and it had great iron teeth: it devoured and brake in pieces, and stamped the residue with the feet of it: and it was diverse from all the beasts that were before it; and it had ten horns."*

Revelation 13:1-2 *"And I stood upon the sand of the sea, and saw a beast rise up out of the sea, having seven heads and ten horns, and upon his horns ten crowns, and upon his heads the name of blasphemy. And the beast which I saw was like unto a leopard, and his feet were as the feet of a bear, and his mouth as the mouth of a lion: and the dragon gave him his power, and his seat, and great authority."*

In Daniel 2, Nebuchadnezzar dreamt the four kingdoms of the world as precious metals in the form of a statue. He was the head of gold, and of course, quite happy about it; politicians view power in terms of wealth and riches (metals). The Persians were silver; the Greeks were brass, and Rome was iron. The Revived Roman Empire is part iron and part clay.

Daniel 7 reveals the same world empires, but God describes them as wild beasts. God sees things differently than man, and it's interesting here that He views the kingdoms of the world as wild beasts that cannot be tamed. As time passes, the beast grows bigger and requires more sustenance than the year before. This can be seen in the common practice of increased taxes but decreased citizens' rights that governments inherently evolve into. We can certainly see that this has taken place here in America. With the country over twenty-one trillion dollars in debt and a government that is growing faster than the private sector; bad things are in our future.

Revelation 13 describes the kingdom of Antichrist and how it will have qualities from each of the four kingdoms of the past. John records them backwards in Revelation 13 because he is looking from the Tribulation back to Babylon. Remember, this final kingdom is a renewal of the Roman Empire.

Satan is also likened unto a wild beast, a dragon. He gives these kingdoms their power. The final kingdom with all the diversity and cultural manifestations of the prior world kingdoms, must be in place and ready to be ruled BEFORE the rapture. A covenant is going to be confirmed between Israel and the Antichrist immediately after the rapture. Since that is the case, then obviously Israel must be in their homeland and seeking peace.

These events are *all* in place today. God is preparing the world for the coming of the Antichrist and His kingdom. The clock is ticking; I believe that time is near.

World Kingdoms Chart

Please view the following chart which illustrates the kingdoms of the world from the time of Daniel until the final One World Kingdom of the Antichrist and the return of Jesus.

In summary, Daniel 2 is Nebuchadnezzar's dream of the world's kingdoms described as man sees them, as precious metals. Daniel 7 describes those same world kingdoms as they really are, as wild beasts that cannot be tamed or controlled. (NOTE: The Founding Fathers implied that the Constitution was to be "chains about the ankles" to restrain the beast we call government.) Revelation 13 lists the same kingdoms viewed from the Tribulation going backwards in history.

Simplified Chart of Word Kingdoms

World Kingdom	Daniel 2	Daniel 7	Revelation 13
1. Babylon Daniel's day 605 B.C.	Head of Gold	Lion with eagle's wings	Mouth of lion
2. Media-Persia 536 B.C.	Chest and arms of silver	Bear	Feet of bear
3. Greece 322 B.C Alex the Great!	Belly and thigh of brass	Leopard Four wings	Like Leopard
4. Rome 63 B.C.	Legs of iron	Dreadful beast	A Beast
5. Antichrist Revived Roman Empire	Feet of iron and clay (ten toes)	Ten horns	Ten horns
6. Christ's Kingdom	Stone cut out without hands	Everlasting kingdom	

More Signs of the Global Kingdom

Besides the rise of Satan's counterfeit trinity, other signs point to the nearing of the revised Roman Empire, but take heart! These signs are not a surprise to God, and they shouldn't surprise us! They need to be in place for the end-time scenario to take place. Consider the following:

1. Cashless Economic System

It is assumed that during the Tribulation there will be a cashless system put in place. We come to this assumption because at the mid-point of the Tribulation, the Antichrist institutes the "mark of the Beast." It is decreed that no financial commerce can take place without this mark. The mark shows allegiance to Antichrist and his global system, and gives permission to exist. The number is 666.

Revelation 13:15-18 *"And he had power to give life unto the image of the beast, that the image of the beast should both speak, and cause that as many as would not worship the image of the beast should be killed. And he causeth all, both small and great, rich and poor, free and bond, to receive a mark in their right hand, or in their foreheads: And that no man might buy or sell, save he that had the mark, or the name of the beast, or the number of his name. Here is wisdom. Let him that hath understanding count the number of the beast: for it is the number of a man; and his number is Six hundred threescore and six.*

Mark of the Beast - 666

When a person accepts the "mark of the beast," he is placing his trust in the Antichrist just as a person would place their trust in Jesus. It is not something that can be forced upon a person; it is an act of the will. If you think about it, the system of a cashless society is already here. If you use a credit card, you are part of it!

Most of the commerce of the world is already being done over the internet without any physical cash being traded.

Many of us use credit/debit cards to pay bills, buy gas or eat at a restaurant. Though we can still use cash, the government has put restrictions on how much cash can be used in one day before red flags are sent to the FBI and you become the suspect of a crime. They claim $10,000 is the trigger point but rest assured, they are watching even smaller transactions.

Cash is on the way out – and fast! With today's modern printers, it is getting so much easier to counterfeit. I suspect that before much longer, the government will make an announcement that "for the good of all" we must discontinue the use of cash. There will be very little resistance to it. I suspect they will give a ninety-day grace period for everyone to convert their cash to digits on a computer screen. Do not panic, most of your wealth is already a digit on a computer.

Microchip implants, computer ID chips placed under human skin, are already being tested with great success. The precursor to the chip is the swiping of our smartphone at the register. For some years now, the credit card prepared us for the cashless society. Credit cards and cash and even your smartphone, can be lost or stolen; an implanted microchip cannot. Most people are anxious for the chip or will be when it comes. The world of commerce is ready for these advancements now.

2. Diverse Seed

Note the use of the terms 'mixed' and 'diverse' in the following scriptures:

Daniel 2:41-43 *"And whereas thou sawest the feet and toes, part of potters' clay, and part of iron, the kingdom shall be divided; but there shall be in it of the strength of the iron, forasmuch as thou sawest the iron mixed with miry clay. And as the toes of the feet were part of iron, and part of clay, so the kingdom shall be partly strong, and partly broken. And whereas thou sawest iron mixed with miry clay, they shall mingle themselves with the seed of men: but they shall not cleave one to another, even as iron is not mixed with clay."*

Daniel 7:7 *"After this I saw in the night visions, and behold a fourth beast, dreadful and terrible, and strong exceedingly; and it had great iron teeth: it devoured and brake in pieces, and stamped the residue with the feet of it: and it was diverse from all the beasts that were before it; and it had ten horns."*

Daniel 7:23 *"Thus he said, The fourth beast shall be the fourth kingdom upon earth, which shall be diverse from all kingdoms, and shall devour the whole earth, and shall tread it down, and break it in pieces."*

Look carefully at what is underlined here. The fourth kingdom is the Roman Empire and it has ten toes in Chapter 2, and ten horns in Chapter 7. Remember, Daniel 2 and 7 are the same world kingdoms. These passages speak of the final kingdom: the ten toes on the feet of the statue and the ten horns in the head of the beast. In other words, the passage is revealing that the fifth and final kingdom comes out of the fourth Roman Empire. It is important that you understand this point. The Antichrist' kingdom is a revived Roman European kingdom that *we are in right now!*

We call it the Revived Roman Empire, and it is the one world kingdom headed up by Antichrist during the Tribulation.

Notice this fifth kingdom, which is the kingdom during the Tribulation, is divided; meaning there is division. Its' iron is mixed with miry clay which shows weakness. It is said to be diverse, showing it is made up of different types of people.

We also see "*...they shall mingle themselves with the seed of men: but they shall not cleave one to another, even as iron is not mixed with clay.*" The last kingdom is made up of all the qualities of the first four kingdoms. In other words, it has many ethnic and cultural differences and customs. After all, it is a kingdom made up of the whole world. Because of this, there will be a diversity of languages and an array of differing opinions and values. Does this sound like what is going on in Europe right now? It is happening in America, too.

Immigration to America used to require assimilation into society by acquiring a skill and learning to speak English. This is no longer the case today or for the recent past. As a result, we are seeing the wisdom of what God conveyed in the

Scriptures many years ago:

Diversity in language and culture does not strengthen a country or its population.

Diversity weakens; that is the truth of God. I am not talking about being racist; I am talking about the language, religious and cultural differences that do not mix. Look what happened at the Tower of Babel. In order to counter the evil that was taking place there, God changed the languages to stop the work and to separate the people. Today, Europe is falling apart because of diversity and America is not far behind.

3. Global Institutions

Lastly, the strong emergence in our culture of the United Nations, the World Bank, the International Money Fund, and the European Union---all are signs pointing to a one world order.

There are NATO police forces and soldiers and we even have the World Council of Churches. Every possible situation is in place to usher in the rule of the Antichrist. God has orchestrated a world system perfectly in order for Satan to rule. Can you hear that clock ticking?

Where Does America Fit In? Who is The Babylon of The End Times?

The United States of Babylon

There is a lot of debate and confusion today about who is Babylon in the end-times. Some believe that ancient Babylon in Iraq must be restored to fulfill this role in the Tribulation; others believe Turkey is the seat of Babylon. Traditionally it is believed to be the Revived Roman Empire, but what about America?

Does the USA fade away, or do we have a role to play in the end-times?

I believe America fulfills the role of Babylon and heads up the Revised Roman Empire during the Tribulation. Please allow me to offer sound Biblical reasoning as to why I hold to this position.

Much confusion about Babylon exists because there are three Babylons to contend with in Scripture.

Once you grasp this important fact, it will forever change the way you look at it in the Bible. Let's begin our journey into the study of Babylon by first realizing there are not one, but three Babylons.

The Three Babylons

1. Literal Babylon - is a desert in Iraq, it would take decades to develop it into the Babylon of the end-times mentioned in Scripture. Some prophecy teachers believe that it must be rebuilt before end-time events take place.

2. Figurative Babylon - can be any place that has the attributes that Babylon possessed in ancient times. Babylon goes all the way back to Nimrod in Genesis 11 and existed at the time of the building of the Tower of Babel. Many of the cultic symbols we see in the world as well as some churches today are rooted in ancient Babylon. Let me give an example of using a city in a figurative sense:

Revelation 11:8 *"And their dead bodies shall lie in the street of the great city, which spiritually is called Sodom and Egypt, where also our Lord was crucified."*

This passage is speaking of Jerusalem, but is calling it Egypt and Sodom in a figurative sense. This puts a graphic description in the mind of the reader. Sodom and Egypt describe the atmosphere of Jerusalem during the Tribulation. Sodom gives us a picture of the gross immorality, and Egypt gives us the picture of idolatry.

3. Prophetic Babylon - is to speak of it as it relates to future end-time events. This is the interpretation we want to dwell on in this discourse.

Babylon is used figuratively and prophetically at the same time to show the religious and political qualities of the final kingdom.

Prophetic Babylon can be confusing because it consists of two separate entities. Revelation 17 is Religious Babylon, and Revelation 18 is Political Babylon.

Church & State

Scripture uses the word "Babylon" to describe the One World Church as well as the One World Political System, which are two different entities of one Kingdom. You could look at it like the United States Congress in Washington. It is one body made up of two entities, the House of Representatives and the Senate. Each has its own leaders, rules, and members, yet together they make up one body – the Congress.

These two entities of Babylon are spoken of in a prophetic sense in the book of Revelation with Chapter 17 speaking of

Religious Babylon, and Chapter 18 Political Babylon. Like Congress, each has its own leaders, and is in different locations, yet are one.

The Antichrist is the head of the political entity of Babylon. The false prophet is the head of the religious entity of Babylon.

Revelation 17 is the fall of Religious Babylon.

Revelation 17:1-6 *"[1]And there came one of the seven angels which had the seven vials, and talked with me, saying unto me, Come hither; I will shew unto thee the judgment of the great whore that sitteth upon many waters: [2]With whom the kings of the earth have committed fornication, and the inhabitants of the earth have been made drunk with the wine of her fornication. [3]So he carried me away in the spirit into the wilderness: and I saw a woman sit upon a scarlet coloured beast, full of names of blasphemy, having seven heads and ten horns. [4]And the woman was arrayed in purple and scarlet colour, and decked with gold and precious stones and pearls, having a golden cup in her hand full of abominations and filthiness of her fornication: [5]And upon her forehead was a name written,* ***MYSTERY, BABYLON THE GREAT, THE MOTHER OF HARLOTS AND ABOMINATIONS OF THE EARTH.*** *[6]And I saw the woman drunken with the blood of the saints, and with the blood of the martyrs of Jesus: and when I saw her, I wondered with great admiration."*

Chapter 17 is a pause at the end of the Tribulation, revealing the fall of the One World Religious system. This will take place during the pouring out of the last plagues on the earth, the seven vial judgments of Revelation 16.

Many believe it is the Catholic Church that will head up the

One World religious system with the Pope filling the role of the False Prophet. Consider a few reasons below:

1. In verses 1 and 2 of our text, we see that *"...the great whore..."* is yoked with kings and nations meaning it is yoked with politics. The Vatican is considered a state, and has ambassadors in nearly every country, including America. In October 2017, Newt Gingrich's wife, Callista, was approved in the U.S. Senate as ambassador to the Vatican.

Constantine merged the state of Rome with the Catholic Church in 313 A.D. This alliance opened the door to the pagan doctrines of: worshiping Mary as the queen of Heaven, purgatory, holy water, candles, a celibate priesthood, and many other pagan beliefs. Remember, Rome was a world kingdom that God describes as a wild beast. To merge a church with a wild beast creates a monster! The Catholic Church helped Hitler rise to power in the 1930's, which was made public a few years ago, and the Pope subsequently apologized.

2. We see the roots of Catholicism way back in Genesis 10 and 11, in the story of Nimrod and the tower of Babel, which is Babylon. Babel, or Babylon, was more than a city, it was a political system of government that has never died. Babylon is still at the root of Catholicism today.

3. Rome is known as the City of the Seven Hills (Revelation 17:9).

4. Revelation 17:4 speaks of the woman being clothed with purple and scarlet: the colors of the bishops and cardinals today.

5. In Revelation 17:3, we see that this woman sits upon the beast which is symbolic of religion and politics mixed together. The Catholic Church is very political even today.

6. In Revelation 17:4, we see that this religious system is very wealthy. There is no doubt, the Catholic Church is worth billions of dollars. The Vatican alone is priceless. I walked through it back in the early 1980's and saw the golden tapestries. There is not any other religious system on the earth that comes close to the wealth of the Catholic Church.

7. Maybe the greatest proof of all is Revelation 17:6, where we see *"...the great whore..."* is drunken with the blood of God's people. It is a historical fact that the Catholic Church is responsible for the slaughter of countless Christians.

Revelation 17:6 *"And I saw the woman drunken with the blood of the saints, and with the blood of the martyrs of Jesus: and when I saw her, I wondered with great admiration."*

Revelation 18 is the fall of Political Babylon.

Look at some of the places I highlighted in the following passage. Does this sound like the description of a desert in Iraq? Does it sound like London or Paris? Would you consider with me that this has all the characteristics of America?

Revelation 18 has all the characteristics of America

Revelation 18: 1-18 *"And after these things I saw another angel come down from heaven, having great power; and the earth was lightened with his glory.* [2] *And he cried mightily with a strong voice, saying,* ***Babylon the great is fallen, is fallen****, and is become the habitation of devils, and the hold of every foul spirit, and a cage of every unclean and hateful bird.* [3] ***For all nations have drunk of the wine of the wrath of her fornication, and the kings of the earth have committed fornication with her, and the merchants of the earth are***

waxed rich through the abundance of her delicacies." [5] *"For* ***her sins*** *have reached unto heaven, and God hath remembered her iniquities."* [9] *"And* ***the kings of the earth, who have committed fornication and lived deliciously with her****, shall bewail her, and lament for her, when they shall see the smoke of her burning,* [10] *standing afar off for the fear of her torment, saying,* ***Alas, alas, that great city Babylon, that mighty city!*** *for in one hour is thy judgment come.* [11] *And the merchants of the earth shall weep and mourn over her;* ***for no man buyeth their merchandise any more:"*** [15] *"The* ***merchants of these things, which were made rich by her****, shall stand afar off for the fear of her torment, weeping and wailing,* [16] *and saying,* ***Alas, alas, that great city,*** *that was clothed in fine linen, and purple, and scarlet, and decked with gold, and precious stones, and pearls!* [17] *For in one hour so great riches is come to nought.* ***And every shipmaster, and all the company in ships, and sailors, and as many as trade by sea, stood afar off,*** [18] ***and cried when they saw the smoke of her burning, saying, What city is like unto this great city!"***

Political Babylon is the final One World System. It is the Revived Roman Empire made up of the ten toes that I believe has its seat here in America. The ten toes are the Revived Roman Empire, not literal Babylon. According to Revelation 13, the final kingdom of Antichrist will consist of an empire made up of attributes of Babylon, Persia, Greece, and Rome. The Roman Empire is still here, and we are a part of it. It will be revived soon. America came from England and is the lion's whelp. We are Europe! Our financial and judicial systems are all rooted in Europe. We are the financial center of the world.

The United Nations is in America because we ARE the United Nations!

There are not many merchants and shipman doing business with literal Babylon, and nobody is going to weep over her if she falls. It is not Turkey that is being referenced in the passage. America is the 'milk cow' for the entire economic world! When she falls, the merchants of the world will weep and wail! She fits the description in Revelation 18 perfectly! We saw a little glimpse of this in 2008 when the big financial crash hit. Remember the fall of Lehman Brothers and General Motors and others? The entire world began to crumble financially because of the crisis here in the USA. That is just a small taste of what is coming for the world.

The political and religious system of Babylon is alive and well in the world.

Babylon never fully died. Its religious principles and its tentacles reach into the entire world. The One World System is already here; the cashless society is already here. For the most part the world is already being run by the globalist elite right here in the USA.

One day soon the Babylonian system will take over the world and probably from right here under our noses.

Things are changing fast, we are in the last of the last days! The fifth and final kingdom is at the door. Daniel's clock is ticking down. We can see it all around us.

Babylon is a philosophy, 'a system', more so than a physical location.

Everything in Israel revolved around the harvest in Bible days.

The Harvest Is A Ticking Clock

The winds are blowing, the leaves are changing and there is a chill in the air as autumn fast approaches. There is a great harvest coming and it will be huge! I am not referring to the changes and transitions that occur from summer to fall seasons; I am speaking about the rapture of the church on God's prophetic calendar. The signs of the coming of the end-times are all around us. A person would have to be blind to not see them. Just as we can see the leaves changing color, and feel the cool winds begin to blow, we can sense the season of the end-times. Paul did say "*That day shall not overtake you as a thief.*"

Just as a farmer knows when the harvest is ready, so, too, can a student of prophecy sense the timing of the return of the Lord. The harvest is a type of the rapture which is part of a three-fold bodily resurrection that is fast approaching. It is a ticking clock that is nearing midnight. The storm clouds can be seen on the horizon, the frigid cold front is moving in, and *it's time for the crops to be gathered into the barn*!

A farmer may not know the day or hour of the harvest, but he certainly knows the season!

The harvest in Biblical Israel holds a prophetic lesson for us concerning both the resurrection, and especially the rapture. One of the great misconceptions today is that Christians think the rapture is all about us, when it is not. The rapture is a resurrection of the bodies of *all* the saints through *all* the centuries who have died. Since there are still living saints on the earth when this resurrection occurs, those living saints will go up in the rapture without ever dying, causing folks to think that we are the focus of it all. Don't misunderstand me, I am very happy to leave this world without dying, but as you will learn in the next few pages, we are not the focus.

The rapture involves us but is not necessarily about us.

1 Thessalonians 4:15-17 *"[15]For this we say unto you by the word of the Lord, that we which are alive and remain unto the coming of the Lord shall not prevent them which are asleep. [16]For the Lord himself shall descend from heaven with a shout, with the voice of the archangel, and with the trump of God: and the dead in Christ shall rise first: [17]Then we which are alive and remain shall be caught up together with them in the clouds, to meet the Lord in the air: and so shall we ever be with the Lord."*

Three-fold Harvest

There is so much in the Scriptures about harvesting crops. The parables about sowing, reaping and harvesting of crops all have lessons for us today. Our generation has missed the lessons the harvesting of crops teach. Fewer people grow up on farms today; most live their lives far removed from the agricultural seasons.

The harvest of a crop has an obvious prophetic meaning, since the resurrection is simply a gathering -- or harvest -- of souls.

Just as there are three stages of the harvest in Israel, there are three stages of the resurrection.

This becomes very important in understanding the rapture as you will see shortly. Remember, the resurrection is always speaking of the body, not the soul.

Two Resurrections

Revelation 20:6 *"Blessed and holy is he that hath part in the first resurrection: on such the second death hath no power, but they shall be priests of God and of Christ, and shall reign with him a thousand years."*

This passage speaks of two bodily resurrections. The first is for the saved; the second is for the lost. This takes place after the 1,000-year Kingdom Age at "*The Great White Throne*."

First Resurrection – Three Stages

When an Old Testament saint died, his body went in the ground, his soul and spirit went to Abraham's bosom, as seen in Luke 16:19-31. This is the place called "Paradise" that Christ promised to the thief on the cross in Luke 23:43, which is so misunderstood today.

Man is a three-fold being consisting of a spirit, soul, and body.

1 Thessalonians 5:23 *"And the very God of peace sanctify you wholly; and I pray God your whole spirit and soul and body be preserved blameless unto the coming of our Lord Jesus Christ."*

Note the order in which God places them. The **spirit** is the part of man that can commune or fellowship with God. That is the part of man that is dead at birth and must be regenerated, quickened (made alive) at salvation.

Ephesians 2:1 "*And you hath he quickened, who were dead in trespasses and sins;*"

The **soul** is the seat of the emotions, intellect and reasoning power. The **body** is the flesh that we can see. Man seems to always get the order backwards. Most preachers say it backwards. To us, the order of importance is the body, the soul, and then the spirit. We spend far more time trying to make the **body** (the outward appearance) attractive, than we do improving the **soul or spirit** (the inward man).

When a believer died during the Old Testament, his body went to the grave, and his soul and spirit went to paradise, Abraham's bosom.

God is a Trinity: Father, Son, and Holy Ghost. Jesus is a three-fold being, too. When Jesus was dying he cried out in Luke 23:46, *"...Father, into thy hands I commend my spirit..."* Yet, He told the thief, *"...To day shalt thou be with me in paradise" (Luke 23:43).* The body of our Saviour was placed in a tomb. Where did the Lord go after He paid the sin debt of the world on the cross of Calvary? He went to all three. His Spirit went to the Father, His soul went to Abraham's bosom, and His body went to the grave.

***See the chapter on Paradise, Mystery of the Jubilee, GodsFinalJubilee.com

When Christ paid the penalty for sin and rose from the grave, He became the "first-fruits of the harvest," the first to rise bodily from the dead. There is that word 'harvest' again! He led the Old Testament saints in Paradise to Heaven. This was the first stage of the three-fold harvest/resurrection.

Since Calvary, the **spirit** and **soul** of all believers who die go to Heaven to be with the Lord (Ephesians 4:8-10). What about the **body**? The body lies in the grave until the rapture; all bodies of the saved, both dead and alive will be resurrected. We do not have our resurrected, glorified bodies yet. We will have a glorified body, like Jesus had when He returned to the apostles after His resurrection. This rapture is the main harvest and explains why it is not as much about the "living" as we'd like to think.

The bodily resurrection of all saved souls throughout history is in three stages, figurative of the three stages of harvesting of a crop.

Here is what the Bible teaches us from Jewish traditions of harvest:

First-fruits – This is the first crop of the fields to ripen and is offered up to the Lord. It is figurative (or a type) of Christ; He was the first to rise bodily from the grave.

Main harvest – This is when the *entire* field is ripe and ready to be picked. It is figurative of the rapture, which is the bodily resurrection of all the saints living and dead. This is the part of the harvest the saints are now awaiting. It sure feels like the harvest clock is about to strike midnight.

Gleanings – This is the final harvest which is simply cleaning up the leftovers after the main crop is harvested.

In Biblical tradition, the Jews were required to leave some of the field's crop for the poor and the widows. They would be allowed to come and "glean" in the field, as seen in the book of Ruth. This is figurative of the resurrection/rapture at the end of the Tribulation when Christ, as the conqueror, returns. (Many of our post-tribulation friends confuse the "gleanings" for the "rapture" in Matthew 24.)

This chart illustrates the two resurrections:

Resurrection of the Saved (First Resurrection)	**Resurrection of the Lost (Second Resurrection)**
In Three Stages *1. **Firstfruits: Calvary*** Matthew 27:50-53 I Corinthians 15:17-26 *2. **Main Harvest: Rapture*** Revelation 4:1 I Thessalonians 4:16 I Corinthians 15:51-52 *3. **Gleanings: Second Coming*** Revelation 14:14-17 Note: You can liken this to three stages of harvesting a crop.	Great White Throne Revelation 20:4-5 at end of 1,000-year Millennium. All who are resurrected at this time are lost.

Actual Crop Harvests

We learned that the harvest of a crop in Bible days was in three stages, which are figurative of the three phases of the bodily resurrection. Now let us look at the harvest *itself* and see the important prophetic truths to be learned from the oldest occupation in the world -- farming.

There were three main harvests in Israel each year that revolved around the seven feast days.

1. Barley harvest- during Passover/Firstfruits
2. Wheat harvest- during Pentecost
3. Fruit harvest- during the Fall Feasts

There are prophetic and figurative lessons in each of these harvests. Let's go a little deeper "into the soil" and see why the harvest is a ticking clock that is close to midnight!

I am going to explain the three harvests in reverse order of their actual seasonal times because this lesson's point specifically centers on the timing of the *barley* harvest.

The fruit harvest is prophetic of the harvest at the rapture.

The wheat harvest is prophetic of the Jew and the Gentile grafted together during the Church Age and harvested together in the rapture.

The barley harvest is a type of first-fruits as it is typically the first crop ready. It is harvested during the Feast of Firstfruits, but most importantly, it is a type of Israel.

When you think of barley, think of Israel and the Hebrew people.

Barley Harvest- a Ticking Clock

Remember, the seven feasts revolve around the three harvests. The barley harvest is the *first* of the three feasts, being planted in the late fall-early winter, and ready for harvest in the spring.

These feasts were very important to the Israelites, as their lives revolved around the harvests. Since the barley was the first harvest on the first month of the calendar, it served as a reset button to keep the seasons right. God's perfect calendar is 360 days a year. Our Gregorian calendar is 365¼ days a year. There are only $354^{2/3}$ days on the Jewish lunar calendar compared to our 365¼-day solar calendar; a shortfall of about 11 days a year. That means every three years there is a discrepancy of about 33 days--a month--an *addition* of a month is needed to keep the seasons right. In Bible days, the barley harvest was the clock they would use as a reset every three years in order to keep the ongoing calendar accurate. So, when the calendar was off, what did they do to correct it? Read on:

Leap Month – Adar II

Firstfruits dictated that there *must* be barley during Passover because it was waved before the Lord on the first day of the week after Passover. If the barley was not ready for this feast, then an *entire month would be added to the calendar year*. That's right! This process was called "determining Abib." For many of you, this is something you may have never heard of. Read these scriptures and definitions carefully, and then allow me to explain the process of determining Abib:

Is it Abib or Nisan?

Exodus 13:4 "*This day came ye out in the month **Abib**.*"

Exodus 23:15 "*Thou shalt keep the feast of unleavened bread: thou shalt eat unleavened bread seven days, as I commanded thee, in the time appointed of the month **Abib**; for in it thou camest out from Egypt: and none shall appear before me empty:*"

Exodus 34:18 "*The feast of unleavened bread shalt thou keep. Seven days thou shalt eat unleavened bread, as I commanded thee, in the time of the month **Abib**: for in the month **Abib** thou camest out from Egypt.*"

Deuteronomy 16:*1 "Observe the month of **Abib**, and keep the passover unto the LORD thy God: for in the month of Abib the LORD thy God brought thee forth out of Egypt by night.*"

Nehemiah 2:1 "*And it came to pass in the month **Nisan**, in the twentieth year of Artaxerxes the king, that wine was before him: and I took up the wine, and gave it unto the king. Now I* *had not been beforetime sad in his presence."*

Esther 3:7 "*In the first month, that is, the month* ***Nisan****, in the twelfth year of king Ahasuerus, they cast Pur, that is, the lot, before Haman from day to day, and from month to month, to the twelfth month, that is, the month Adar."*

From Webster's 1828 Dictionary

A'BIB, noun [Heb. swelling, protuberant. To produce the first or early fruit; a full-grown ear of corn.]

The first month of the Jewish ecclesiastical year, also called Nisan. It begins at the spring equinox, and answers to the latter part of March and beginning of April. Its name is derived from the full growth of wheat in Egypt, which took place anciently, as it does now, at that season.

NIS'AN, noun A month of the Jewish calendar, the first month of the sacred year and seventh of the civil year, answering nearly to our March. It was originally called Abib but began to be called Nisan after the captivity.

An Unexpected Revelation

Were you surprised to see these terms mentioned so many times in Scripture? What's their application to this teaching?

I was surprised to learn that God used the word "Abib" instead of the word "Nisan" when He instituted the Passover month for the first time. Most people today use the word Nisan to describe Passover month. Almost every prophecy book you will read uses Nisan. I have several books written by Jewish men and most of them are from the 50's or older and they all used the word Nisan instead of Abib.

So, what is Abib?

Abib is used six times in Scripture. The month Nisan is only used two times. This surprised me even more. I was sure that Nisan was the word that we should use. After further study, I found that, **Abib is the word we should use to describe the first month of the Jewish agricultural calendar.**

From Webster's Dictionary as well as from the context and its usage in the Bible, it is plain to see that, **Abib means to be full-grown or ready for harvest.** It means to be ripe. Are you seeing any prophetic applications here yet? Since Passover is *always* at barley harvest, Abib is speaking of barley.

The month Abib literally means the month of the harvest of the barley.

If the barley is not matured, it cannot be the month Abib. Look again at the six times in Scripture that the word Abib is used. You can see in the context that the Hebrews came out of Egypt in the time of barley harvest. They came out in the month of Abib. If the barley is not ready for harvest, the Levites cannot announce that it is Abib. If you are still confused, I think you will understand after you read a little further:

Determining Abib

This is the ancient practice the Jews used to determine Abib:

On the last day of the twelfth month, called Adar, the priest would observe the barley fields. If the barley was within six to eleven days of harvest, he would announce that it is Abib---it is ready. *In other words, the priest would announce that it is Passover month.* It would then be considered the month Abib AND the first month on their feast calendar. Passover would be just fourteen days away on the full moon.

What if the barley wasn't ready? If it was not, the priest would announce a leap year, the month of Adar II which is a thirteenth month added to reset the calendar. **This is how God ordained that they keep the seasons rightly accounted for** since they only have 354$^{2/3}$ days on their Jewish calendar. Once again, the accumulation of 11 days each year would add up to about a month for every three years. Be patient: there is a huge prophetic lesson here that we will get to shortly! Just make sure you understand the following:

No Barley-No Abib
No Abib-No Passover

Nisan Used Twice

To review, *only twice* the first month of the Jewish calendar is referred to as Nisan. It was named so in Nehemiah and Esther, when the Israelites were at the end of the seventy-year captivity. At that time, there was no temple and the Jews were not keeping the Jewish feasts. They were not able to observe the condition of the barley as most likely there was no barley crop to observe! Therefore, the Passover month was called Nisan. It was still month number one but had *no relation to the ripened barley harvest.*

Dreaming of Barley

The events told in the Bible are not just bedtime stories but are there to teach and enlighten us -- especially in a prophetic context. One such 'story' is in Judges Chapters 6 and 7 where Gideon reveals **a great mystery concerning the cake of barley and the nation of Israel.**

In Judges 6, we read that the children of Israel had rebelled against God. In turn, the Lord delivered the Israelites into the hand of Midian for seven years.

Judges 6:1 *"And the children of Israel did evil in the sight of the LORD: and the LORD delivered them into the hand of Midian seven years."*

That is an interesting time span considering the Tribulation period is seven years and has to do with the judgement of Israel.

A Prophetic Story

There can be little doubt that this story is prophetic of the end-times. It was a time of judgment for Israel, just as the tribulation will be after the church is raptured. In Judges 7, the people repented and cried unto the Lord for mercy. God chose Gideon to deliver the people from the hands of the Midianites and the Amalekites. God cuts Gideon's army down to just three hundred men. These were men seasoned in battle, yet no match for the tens of thousands of enemy soldiers that awaited them in the valley below. As you read the passage, realize it is literal as well as prophetic.

Judges 7:9-15 *"9 And it came to pass the same night, that the LORD said unto him, Arise, get thee down unto the host; for I have delivered it into thine hand. 10 But if thou fear to go down, go thou with Phurah thy servant down to the host: 11 And thou shalt hear what they say; and afterward shall thine hands be strengthened to go down unto the host. Then went he down with Phurah his servant unto the outside of the armed men that were in the host. 12 And the Midianites and the Amalekites and all the children of the east lay along in the valley like grasshoppers for multitude; and their camels were without number, as the sand by the sea side for multitude. 13 And when Gideon was come, behold, there was a man that told a dream unto his fellow, and said, Behold, I dreamed a dream, and, lo* ***, a cake of barley bread tumbled into the host of Midian****, and came unto a tent, and smote it that it fell, and overturned it, that the tent lay along. 14 And his fellow answered and said,* ***This is nothing else save the sword of Gideon the son of Joash, a man of Israel****: for into his hand hath God delivered Midian, and all the host. 15 And it was so, when Gideon heard the telling of the dream, and the interpretation thereof, that he worshipped, and returned into the host of Israel, and said, Arise; for the LORD hath delivered into your hand the host of Midian.*

In verse 9, God commands Gideon to take the three hundred

men and go fight the enemy. God promises to give the victory. However, in verse 10 we see that Gideon has some obvious concerns about winning this battle (I can certainly relate to his concerns). God instructs Gideon to take his servant down to the camp of the Midianites. They went in the dark of night, and just listened outside one of the tents.

The Barley Represents Israel

This is the crux of the story that I want you to get. In verses 13-14 we see that one Midianite is telling his dream to another man inside his tent. He explained that in his dream, a cake of barley rolled into the camp and literally flattened the tent! The other fellow declares, *"...This is nothing else save the sword of Gideon the son of Joash, a man of Israel..."* **The man understood that the barley cake represented Israel,** and that the armies of Midian would be defeated.

The great mystery revealed in the story and understood by the interpreter of the dream is that barley is a type of Israel.

Abib Barley

Remember, the beginning of the month Abib is dependent on the condition of the barley in the field. If the barley was not ripe it was necessary to add a month (Adar II) to reset the calendar. This would usually happen every three years because the Jewish calendar is only 354$^{2/3rd}$ days. They are short eleven days every year. It was vital that the barley be ripe to "*...wave the sheaf before the Lord...*" as instructed in Leviticus.

Leviticus 23:9-11 *"9And the LORD spake unto Moses, saying,*
10Speak unto the children of Israel, and say unto them, When
ye be come into the land which I give unto you, and shall reap the harvest thereof, then ye shall bring a sheaf of the firstfruits of your harvest unto the priest: 11And he shall wave the sheaf

before the LORD, to be accepted for you: on the morrow after the sabbath <u>*the priest shall wave it.*</u>

Customarily, this takes place on feast number three of the seven feasts. It is the Feast of Firstfruits. Remember, Firstfruits takes place on the first day of the week (Sunday), after Passover as explained in Leviticus 23 and is during the barley harvest. **More importantly, if there is no barley ready, the Passover is backed up a month and the calendar is reset.**

The Lord was the first to reset
the Jewish calendar for Abib.

Exodus 12:1-3 *"[1]And the LORD spake unto Moses and Aaron in the land of Egypt, saying, [2]This month shall be unto you the beginning of months: it shall be the first month of the year to you. [3]Speak ye unto all the congregation of Israel, saying, In the tenth day of this month they shall take to them every man a lamb, according to the house of their fathers, a lamb for an house:*

Here, we see that the Lord told Moses that the month we call Abib/Nisan (Passover month), would now be the first month of their year. There can be no doubt that this is Passover month when you see the choosing of a lamb in verse three.

This set a precedent going forward for all time. Passover would be determined by Abib. In other words, when the barley is ripe, it is Abib. Passover will be on the full moon of the fourteenth day of that same month. The timing of all seven feasts is determined by the condition of the barley. Since the barley represents Israel, the lesson is this: **Israel is the key to the resetting of God's prophetic clock!** Do not panic; if the light of this revelation hasn't come on yet, keep reading.

Why did the Jews Stop Using This System?

The simple answer is they were no longer in their land! They were not practicing their feast days! There was no barley harvest to observe!

In their dispersion (diaspora or exile), the Jews had no way to be sure which month was Passover. The barley harvest had to be physically observed by the tribe of Levi. This was very serious in their day. *Everything* depended on the barley harvest. There had to be barley sheaves to wave on the Feast of Firstfruits. They had been commanded to count forty-nine days from Firstfruits to determine Pentecost. *They had to get this right!* If they were not in Israel, there was no way to know if the barley was ripe. And no amount of communication (technology was non-existent then) could make up for it!

So, what did they do regarding an accurate calendar? Over time, the religious leaders came up with a mathematical plan to add in the extra month, so every Jew would know in advance when to celebrate the Passover.

After they were dispersed, this new calendar system worked no matter where a person lived in the world. This is still practiced today. But, to make it perfectly clear: this was not how God planned it. There must be barley before it can be Abib. Passover is determined by the condition of the barley. God ordained it that way. This is how they kept the seasons in check. The Levites were to observe the barley crop before the new moon of the month to determine if the barley would be ready in time for Firstfruits. It was God's reset button to keep the seasons right.

Making the Prophetic Connection

Abib Barley is God's sign to determine the timing of end-time events.

Barley is a type of Israel. Therefore, the condition of the barley/Israel is also how God will determine the season of Abib for the start of end-time events. The condition of Israel is what will determine the time and the season when God hits the reset button for the end of the age.

Israel is what determines the beginning of God's end-time clock.

Israel, being Abib in God's sight, determines the season for the return of Jesus Christ! When the nation of Israel is ready, when Israel is Abib, God will reset the Biblical calendar and the end-time events will be put in motion. I believe God will take out the church in the seventh month following the reset, in the new moon of the seventh month from Abib. It will be the Feast of Trumpets on God's Prophetic Calendar!

Let's Consider: Should we keep Passover?

Let me stop and add this so there is no confusion. For 2,000 years it has not mattered when Passover was on the calendar! Now, before you get upset, let me explain. There are many figurative and spiritual lessons for us to glean from the Passover and the seven feasts. I have shared many of these lessons already. However, when Jesus died on the cross, the God of Heaven tore the veil of the temple from top to bottom. This symbolized the fulfillment of the ceremonial law which pointed to Christ. For 2,000 years, we have been in the Church Age, a parenthesis inserted between the 69th and 70th week of Daniel. In other words, the Old Testament prophets did not see the Church Age.

During this current age, you and I are the temple and are indwelled by the Spirit of God.

Jesus fulfilled all things. Jesus was/is the Passover Lamb. We no longer need to kill a lamb each year. There is no reason for the feasts today. Though I am not against having a

Passover service or blowing the shofar, we are not required to observe the feasts. It is fine for a church to observe them as long as the people know it is only for a remembrance. The spring feasts have all been fulfilled by the Lord Jesus Christ and the veil in the temple was torn in two as a sign that they were fulfilled. Now, with that made clear, what is the significance of the seven feasts and the barley harvest for us today?

The Feasts are a prophetic calendar,
not only what God has done,
but also what God is going to do.

One day soon God will see that Israel is Abib. God will see that His people Israel, the barley, are ready for the harvest. He will see that everything is in place, and Israel is ready to begin their 70th week that was prophesied in Daniel 9:24-27.

I believe the Old Testament clock stopped at the year 3993. After the rapture of the church, it will be the year 5993. At this point there will be seven years remaining to complete 6,000 years. Those seven years remaining will be the 70th week of Daniel that we call the Tribulation. They will complete the 4,000 years of the Old Testament. Look at it this way: those seven years will finish off the Old Testament clock to the year 4000. Add the 2,000 years in the Church Age and 1,000 years in the Kingdom Age, that will complete a perfect 7,000-year earth! When the barley is ripe, God will once again turn His full attention to His people, the Jews.

It is not the church, but Israel
that determines the timing
of end-time events.

Quick Summary…

1. On the new moon of Abib/Nisan when God determines that all things are ready with the nation of Israel, He will hit the reset button. It will be Abib on His prophetic calendar.
2. Seven months to the day from that reset will be the new moon in the month of Tishri. It will be in the fall, and it will be on God's Feast of Trumpets.
3. I believe that will be the day the Lord removes the church and begins the 70th week of Daniel with the confirming of the covenant (Daniel 9:24).
4. It is very likely *not* going to be the Feast of Trumpets on the Jewish calendar used today, because they do not use the system of Abib.

The seven feasts are God's prophetic calendar. An understanding of these seven feasts is the key that unlocks the door to prophecy. These seven feasts take place in seven months of the Jewish calendar. The first four feasts have been fulfilled right to the day by Christ. I believe the final three fall feasts will be fulfilled to the exact day with the rapture and the second coming.

Because we cannot know when Israel is Abib, we will never know the timing of the Rapture!

God has designed a perfect system for keeping the calendar on track. That same system will be used of the Lord to bring about the final series of events leading up to the 70th week.

No man can possibly know the day nor the hour of either the rapture or the Second Coming, because we cannot know which month is Abib each year.

Another Jewel: The Twelve Baskets

There is one more hidden jewel concerning barley that I want you to see before we end this chapter. It is hidden in the familiar story in the following passage.

John 6:1-14 *"After these things Jesus went over the sea of Galilee, which is the sea of Tiberias.* [2]*And a great multitude followed him, because they saw his miracles which he did on them that were diseased.* [3]*And Jesus went up into a mountain, and there he sat with his disciples.* [4]*And the passover, a feast of the Jews, was nigh.* [5]*When Jesus then lifted up his eyes, and saw a great company come unto him, he saith unto Philip, "Whence shall we buy bread, that these may eat?"* [6]*And this he said to prove him: for he himself knew what he would do.* [7]*Philip answered him, "Two hundred pennyworth of bread is not sufficient for them, that every one of them may take a little."* [8]*One of his disciples, Andrew, Simon Peter's brother, saith unto him,* [9]*There is a lad here, which hath five barley loaves, and two small fishes: but what are they among so many?* [10]*And Jesus said, Make the men sit down. Now there was much grass in the place. So the men sat down, in number about five thousand.* [11]*And Jesus took the loaves; and when he had given thanks, he distributed to the disciples, and the disciples to them that were set down; and likewise of the fishes as much as they would.* [12]*When they were filled, he said unto his disciples, "Gather up the fragments that remain, that nothing be lost."* [13]*Therefore they gathered them together, and filled twelve baskets with the fragments of the five barley loaves, which remained over and above unto them that had eaten.* [14]*Then those men, when they had seen the miracle that Jesus did, said, "This is of a truth that prophet that should come into the world."*

Feeding the 5000

What does the barley harvest, Passover and the prophetic calendar have to do with the feeding of the 5,000? First, let's start with some spiritual truths represented in this story:

1. It takes place around the time of the feast of Passover.

2. Passover being nigh explains a great mystery. Note that there are no women and children mentioned at first, though they were there. In Jewish tradition, there were three times during each year that all the Jewish men were required to be in Jerusalem (Deuteronomy 16:16). The Feast of Unleavened Bread was the first occasion beginning at 6:00 P.M., at the end of Passover. Obviously, the men would have to travel and get there ahead of time. It is probably what happened in this passage. It would explain why these 5,000 men are there. The other two feasts are Pentecost and Tabernacles. (Incidentally, that would explain why the multitudes were in Jerusalem in Acts 2 where 3,000 are added to the Lord.)

3. Being the time of Passover explains why the lad has five barley loaves: it's the crop that's in season.

4. In addition to the five loaves of barley, there were two fishes. **That makes seven in all**, God's number of perfection and completeness (credit to my son, Ezekiel, for this one).

5. After everyone had eaten, they gathered up the fragments and filled *twelve* baskets. That is symbolic of the number of Jesus' disciples, and the number of original tribes of Israel.
6. Remember, barley is a type of Israel. We saw that in Judges 7 in the story of Gideon.

7. There is no mention that any of the two fishes were leftover and collected into the baskets. Fish is a symbol of New Testament Christianity and represents the saints.

The Prophetic Lesson revealed…

The five barley loaves are a type of Israel. The two fishes are a type of the New Testament Church. I believe the filling of the twelve baskets with the fragments of the barley is prophetic of the twelve tribes of Israel returning to their land

and being prepared to take part in and fulfill their role in the coming 70th week of Daniel!

When the 12 tribes are Abib (ready), God will remove the two fishes (church) and deal with Israel.

Consider again that there was no mention of any fragments or leftovers to be gathered of the two fishes. The two fishes are a type of the New Testament Christians.

Fate of the Jews after the Rapture

During the seven-year Tribulation, along with redeeming the planet, God will also redeem Israel beginning with the 144,000 Jewish men. Scripture tells us in Revelation 7 that they come from the twelve tribes of Israel (the twelve baskets of barley fragments) and will become believers right at the middle of the 70th week of the Tribulation.

It is the condition of the barley that determines the timing of the end-time events. Right now, the barley and the two fishes serve and dwell together. For nearly 2,000 years the Jews, at least as a nation, have been placed in the background. God revealed to the apostle Paul the mystery of the church and how it would be used to get the Word of God around the world. **In the church, there is no difference between the Jew and the Gentile**. We are one in Christ. The church is made up of born-again people. The Jews were the very foundation of the church. God is not finished with Israel as a nation.
Israel is the barley and God has His eye on them still. Since before 1948, the Jews have been returning to their homeland, just as the Bible said they would. In 1948, Israel officially became a sovereign nation once again after approximately 2,520 years. In 1967, they gained control of Jerusalem in the Six-Day War -- truly a miraculous and historic event. Of the thirteen million Jews on the planet today, more than half of

them are now in Israel. God has greatly prospered and blessed that land.

Very soon, when God determines that the barley (Israel) is ready, the Lord will remove the two fishes and finish gathering together the fragments of the barley into the twelve tribes of Israel! I am convinced it is already happening.

When the barley/Israel is Abib (ripe/ready), the prophetic clock will be reset.

A Final Revelation

"It is interesting to note that after the feeding of the 5,000, the twelve apostles were told to get in a boat and cross the Sea of Galilee. At the mid-point, they found themselves in a storm and were in great turmoil, until the Lord appeared in the fourth watch to rescue them. This is an obvious picture of the Jews recognizing the Messiah at the middle of the 70th week of Daniel." (This from my good friend, Phil Hauser.)

In Bible days, the Levites would determine Abib. In the last days, God will determine Abib.

ISRAEL'S TICKING CLOCK

The nation of Israel is the greatest of all the end-time prophetic signs. It is the most visible *ticking clock* of the seven discussed in this book. Old-time preachers would often say concerning Bible prophecy, "Keep your eyes on Israel."

M.R. DeHann is one of my favorite eschatology writers of the past. He wrote in his book, *The Revelation*, that Israel would one day be back in their land. The book was published in 1946; Israel became a sovereign nation in 1948. Lest you think it was a lucky guess, he also predicted that one day man would break the sound barrier and even land men on the moon. We laugh at that now, but men like DeHaan, Larkin, and others were ahead of their time.

The fact that Israel exists today is one of the biggest signs of the times you could ever witness! For many centuries it was only wishful thinking, but today it is a miracle! Make no mistake: *the end-time events are about Israel, not the Church.*

Israel is not only a ticking clock pointing to midnight, it is a ticking time-bomb trumpeting out a warning to all who have "ears to hear."

Prophetic Indicators

Let us start by establishing three events concerning Israel that MUST be in place for the rapture to occur.

1. Israel must be in their land.

Daniel 9:27 shows they will have the Temple in place.

2. Israel must be in need of a peace treaty.

Daniel 9:27 *"And he shall confirm the covenant with many for one week: and in the midst of the week he shall cause the sacrifice and the oblation to cease, and for the overspreading of abominations he shall make it desolate, even until the consummation, and that determined shall be poured upon the desolate."*

3. Israel must be ready to build a temple.

2 Thessalonians 2:4 *"Who opposeth and exalteth himself above all that is called God, or that is worshipped; so that he as God sitteth in the temple of God, shewing himself that he is God."*

When the Antichrist declares himself to be god, *he is in the Temple.* That means, Israel must not only be in their land, but also have already built the Temple by mid-Tribulation.

A light study of both recent history and news headlines indicate the fulfillment of all three indicators! Can you hear the clock ticking?

Now, let us look at a little history. In doing so, remember when you speak of Israel you are referring to the nation. The term Hebrew speaks of the natural-born race, and the term Jew refers to the religion of Judaism. (One can visit the nation of Israel and even convert to the Jewish faith; but one can only be born into the Hebrew race.)

When the Nation of Israel Began

Genesis 12:1-2 *"Now the LORD had said unto Abram, Get thee out of thy country, and from thy kindred, and from thy father's house, unto a land that I will shew thee: And I will make of thee a great nation, and I will bless thee, and make thy name great; and thou shalt be a blessing:"*

This is the account of Israel which began with Abraham. We also see this confirmed clearly in Stephen's discourse to the Jewish leaders in the New Testament. He began by telling of Abraham and ended with the account of Moses leading a rebellious people through the desert to Caanan.

Acts 7:2 *"And he said, Men, brethren, and fathers, hearken; The God of glory appeared unto our father Abraham, when he was in Mesopotamia, before he dwelt in Charran,"*

Through Israel, God blessed the world with three things:

1. The Saviour (Isaiah 9:6)
2. Salvation- "salvation is of the Jews"
3. The Scriptures- "the oracles of God"

Genesis 12:3 *"And I will bless them that bless thee, and curse him that curseth thee: and in thee shall all families of the earth be blessed."*

I'd just like to emphasize here the great blessing we have of

God's Word, the Bible. **It is the very oracles of God, who is the Ancient of Days, the Creator of the universe.** You and I cannot sit at the feet of Jesus or hear Him teach from a boat at the Sea of Galilee. We cannot listen as He shares a parable about a prodigal son, nor can we hear Him preach from the Mount of Olives. But let me admonish you, dear friends, that you and I have something that nobody had in Jesus' day.

In fact, you and I have something that nobody had for 5,600 years: the Holy Scriptures, from Genesis to Revelation! We have the complete canon of Scripture that we can hold in our hands. Before the 1600's, that wasn't possible. In that alone, the nation of Israel has blessed us beyond all measure!

Now let's itemize, for the sake of the 'ticking clock,' how the three prophetic indicators are being fulfilled today -- in our generation.

1. FULFILLED! Israel Returns to Their Land

When Jesus spoke of **the fig tree**, it was as a type of the nation of Israel:

Matthew 24:32-34 *Now learn a parable of the fig tree; When his branch is yet tender, and putteth forth leaves, ye know that summer is nigh: So likewise ye, when ye shall see all these things, know that it is near, even at the doors. Verily I say unto you, This generation shall not pass, till all these things be fulfilled.*

This passage is a prophecy about the restoration of the nation of Israel. Just as significant, the mention of "generation" speaks to the **timing** (or 'ticking clock') of when the season of end-time events would occur after the statehood of Israel was declared. *This prophecy was fulfilled in 1948 when the Jews returned to their homeland after WWII and declared their sovereignty.*

I propose that the fig tree "took root" in 1948, and "budded" in 1967, after the Six-Day War, when they acquired Jerusalem. This is a prophetic mystery that few could comprehend prior to 1967.

Ezekiel's Bones:

Ezekiel speaks of the restoration of Israel to its national statehood. The story is self-explanatory in the text:

Ezekiel 37:3-7 *"And he said unto me, Son of man, can these bones live? And I answered, O Lord GOD, thou knowest. Again he said unto me, Prophesy upon these bones, and say unto them, O ye dry bones, hear the word of the LORD. Thus saith the Lord GOD unto these bones; Behold, I will cause breath to enter into you, and ye shall live: And I will lay sinews upon you, and will bring up flesh upon you, and cover you with skin, and put breath in you, and ye shall live; and ye shall know that I am the LORD. So I prophesied as I was commanded: and as I prophesied, there was a noise, and behold a shaking, and the bones came together, bone to his bone."*

An important fact to point out here is that Ezekiel was a prophet to Israel before and during the Babylonian captivity, which was when Israel lost its statehood.

No other nation in the history of the world has ever ceased to exist and then years later recovered their statehood.

God's Orchestration of Israel's Statehood

Great Britain began the process for the restoration of Israel with the Balfour Agreement in 1917. The U.N. (and Britain) deeded the land of Israel to the Jews. On May 14, 1948, David Ben-Gurion read the Israeli Declaration of Independence which declared Israel to be an independent state. That same day, the United States recognized Israel as an independent and sovereign nation.

Israel obtained Jerusalem in 1967, after the miraculous Six-Day War. I lean towards this event as "*The fig tree buddeth*" fulfillment of Matthew 24:32; for what is Israel without Jerusalem?

It cannot be emphasized enough: *Israel is the only nation in all of history that lost its statehood and then gained it back.* God's hand of protection and guidance has been on the Jewish people throughout all of history and Israel will once again take center stage as end-time events and the Tribulation take place. Therefore, Israel is a ticking clock that should be watched closely!

Israel's History Replete with Numerology

Let us look at more history and numerology of Israel. Together they will help us understanding the end-times and the ticking of Israel's clock.

There are approximately 2,520 years from the captivity in Babylon to 1948, when Israel became a nation.

Israel returned to statehood and their land in 1948. Yes, they had rebuilt the temple at a point in their history (Ezra, Nehemiah), but *no*t as a sovereign nation. When Jesus walked among them, it was in Jerusalem and Israel, but they were under Roman rule and not a sovereign state. My point here is that Israel became a sovereign state *after* 2,520 years, and that is an interesting number in Scripture as I will show in a moment.

If you're not familiar with the seventy-year Babylonian captivity, you would benefit from a serious study on it. There is so much of the Bible that revolves around this time. The entire books of Ezekiel and Jeremiah take place just before and after Nebuchadnezzar conquered Jerusalem. The attack occurred in two stages, dating approximately 605-586 B.C.

The book of Daniel begins with a young Hebrew boy being taken into captivity. The last half of this book, as well as Ezra, Nehemiah, and Esther are all post-captivity books. When you understand these time periods, the Bible will begin to make so much more sense to you.

Connecting the historical events

The Jews were in captivity for 70 years, which ended when Persia defeated Babylon and became the world power under Cyrus. The Jews were given freedoms and allowed to rebuild the city, but they were not a sovereign state existing separate from the dictatorships of world empires. In 70 A.D., the last Jewish temple was destroyed by the Romans. The Jews were scattered world-wide and suffered unending persecution. In 1948, they again became a nation after 2,520 years had ticked off the clock.

The 2,520 years is one giant "Sabbatical cycle!"

Remember from our earlier study that a Sabbatical cycle is 7 years, or 2,520 days. The Tribulation, too, will last 2,520 days; two halves each 1,260 days. Look at it this way: the period of 2,520 days is like a huge Sabbatical cycle.

More Interesting 2,520 Numerology

The following are some very interesting variables of the number 2,520 using God's prophetic 360-day calendar. Note, too, how the number seven, God's number of completion, plays in so seamlessly:

-7,000 years is equal to 2,520,000 days.
-2,520,000 days is equal to 360,000 weeks.
-70 years is equal to 25,200 days.
-25,200 days equals 3,600 weeks.
-7 years is equal to 2,520 days.
-2,520 days is equal to 360 weeks.
-2,520 years is equal to 360 weeks of years.
-2,520 weeks is equal to 49 years. (Jubilee cycle)
-7,000 years is the whole history of the earth.
-70 years is the length of the Babylonian Captivity.

Even God's creation revolves around this special number. For instance, the moon is 252,000 miles from earth at its apogee (when it is furthest from earth). And in mathematics: the smallest number that is divisible by the numbers 1-10 is **2520**.

Anglican scholar and theologian, E.W. Bullinger, called **2,520** *"chronological perfection!"*

2. FULFILLED! Israel is in need of a peace treaty for protection from their enemies.

Read any headline on Middle-East events and you'll realize that Israel is, once again, surrounded by enemies. This time, by powers outside of her borders, as well as those on them: Russia, Iran, Turkey, Syria, Palestinian and terrorist groups, and more. That is a lot of enemies---tiny Israel could be annihilated in an hour!

This is a critical situation that will force Israel into signing a peace treaty, which could happen any day. (NOTE: it doesn't have to take place before the rapture.) If you've studied the book of Revelation, you understand that Israel's enemies will not destroy her but instead will be used by God to ultimately bring Israel to acknowledge Jesus as their Messiah. The question is, *when* will God initiate the final chapter?

Scripture tells us that Israel is going to confirm a covenant (peace treaty) with the Antichrist after the church is raptured. Current events seem to be putting everything in place for this covenant. The enemies are threatening; a peace treaty is imminent: the clock is ticking down.

3. FULFILLED! Israel is ready to build a temple.

For decades, the Jewish people have been preparing to re-build the Temple. From architectural plans and materials to furnishings and sacrificial artifacts, *everything* needed for rebuilding the temple is ready; and exactly to Biblical specs as governed by *The Temple Institute* in Jerusalem.

The only thing standing in the way has been the dispute over land on which to build. The Jews must build on the old temple site which is unfortunately claimed by other powers in the city. It is a point of contention that just may be settled in the peace treaty.

According to Mathew 24, the temple must be ready right after the rapture. It is possible the Antichrist will, in fact, build the temple for the Jews as part of the peace treaty. However events play out, the temple could be constructed in a matter of weeks!

A Timely Temple Preparation

As an example of the temple preparation, recently a news story from Jerusalem focused on "a red heifer without spot" as stated in this passage of Scripture:

Numbers 19:1-3 *"And the LORD spake unto Moses and unto Aaron, saying, This is the ordinance of the law which the LORD hath commanded, saying, Speak unto the children of*

Israel, that they bring thee a *<u>red heifer without spot</u>, wherein is no blemish, and upon which never came yoke: And ye shall give her unto Eleazar the priest, that he may bring her forth without the camp, and one shall slay her before his face:"*

Following is the actual news article:

Henry Holloway Published 8th September 2018

The Temple Institute announced the birth of an entirely red female calf that "brings the promise of reinstating Biblical purity to the world".

Red heifers feature in end times tales in both Christianity and Judaism.

The cow's birth and sacrifice is said to proceed the construction of the <u>Third Temple in Jerusalem</u>.

And the Third Temple's construction – following the destruction of the previous two – heralds the arrival of the Jewish Messiah.

While some Evangelical Christian theologians have linked the building of the Third Temple to Judgement Day.

Rabbi Chain Richman, director of the Temple Institute, hailed the red heifer's birth as suggestions the time could be right for the Third Temple.

The Temple Institute announced the birth of the red heifer on their YouTube page with the video "Red heifer candidate born in Israel".

It includes a video of the red calf and its mother – revealing "a perfectly red heifer was born in the land of Israel".

The cow went under "extensive examination by rabbinical experts" who confirmed she is a "viable candidate for the Biblical red heifer".

The newborn red heifer was verified by a board of rabbis from the Temple Institute as fulfilling the prophesied requirements.

Prophecy in the Hebrew Bible states the cow must be red "without blemish", must not have worked.

It is claimed there have only been nine true red heifers – and the 10th will herald the construction of the Third Temple.

The Temple Institute believes a red heifer will be needed to be scarified to complete the ritual of purification for the temple – heralding the coming of the Jewish Messiah.

Red heifers have previously been found by the organization – who have then disqualified them for not meeting prophetic standards.

One was found in 1999 but was disqualified for being male – and a second was born in 2002, which was found to have a patch of white hair.

Writing on the Temple Institute's website, Rabbi Caimen said: "Does this perhaps mean that the appearance of a red heifer in these waning end times is an indication, a forerunner of the appearance of the Messiah himself, who will officiate at its preparation?

"If there has been no red heifer for the past 2,000 years, perhaps it is because the time was not right; Israel was far from being ready.

"But now, what could it mean for the times we live in, to have the means for purification so close at hand?"

He added: "We cannot help but wonder and pray: If there are now red heifers... is ours the era that will need them?"

Evangelical Christians believe the construction of the Third Temple all herald their own end times prophecy.

The prophecy has even been linked to the US President Donald Trump moving the US Embassy to Jerusalem.

Rabbi Hillel Weiss said he believes Trump's decision over the embassy is the first stage of bringing about the end of days.

Henry Holloway Published 8th September 2018
https://www.dailystar.co.uk/news/weird-news/728262/bible-prophecy-hebrew-red-heifer-messiah-jewish-christianity-israel-jerusalem-third-temple

Isn't it fascinating to see ancient prophesies come to life? Here's another one:

The Dam on the Euphrates River

Here, the Bible speaks of the Euphrates River drying up and the "kings of the east" crossing to invade Israel:

Revelation 16:12 *"And the sixth angel poured out his vial upon the great river Euphrates; and the water thereof was dried up, that the way of the kings of the east might be prepared."*

These "kings" can only be referring to the country of China. Right now, the Ataturk Dam is in place to control waters of the region and has the ability to actually stop the Euphrates from flowing. Literally with a push of a button this dam will, indeed, dry up the waters and make a way for the soldiers of China, the prophesied "*kings from the east!"*

> **Ataturk Dam**, dam on the Euphrates River in southeastern Turkey, the centrepiece of the Southeastern Anatolia Project. The Ataturk Dam is the largest in a series of 22 dams and 19 hydroelectric stations built on the Euphrates and Tigris rivers in the 1980s and '90s in order to provide irrigation water and hydroelectricity to arid southeastern Turkey. Completed in 1990, the Ataturk Dam is one of the world's largest earth-and-rock fill dams, with an embankment 604 feet (184 metres) high and 5,971 feet (1,820 metres) long. Water impounded by the dam is fed to power-generating units at Şanlıurfa that have a capacity of 2,400 megawatts. From there the water is gravity-fed to vast irrigation networks in the Harran Plain and elsewhere in the vicinity.
> "Ataturk Dam". *Encyclopædia Britannica. Encyclopædia Britannica Online.* Encyclopædia Britannica Inc., 2018. Web. 28 Sep. 2018 <https://www.britannica.com/topic/Ataturk-Dam>.

In Summary

Our generation--the one observing and praying for the return of Jesus today--has witnessed the fulfillment of exciting Biblical prophesies regarding Israel.

Ezekiel 20:34 *"And I will bring you out from the people, and will gather you out of the countries wherein ye are scattered, with a mighty hand, and with a stretched out arm, and with fury poured out."*

We have seen God orchestrate the miraculous rebirth of Israel by bringing the Jews back to their homeland, causing them to flourish, and to prepare for a new temple. We've watched as Israel's enemies have surrounded and threatened her almost to the point of war, forcing her to consider a soon-coming peace treaty.

God promised to bring the Jews back to their homeland and *He has kept his promise.*

Friends, this has all taken place in our generation. Men of prior generations saw and wrote about these events, but they have been fulfilled in ours. Israel is in their land and in desperate need of peace. They will resume the temple worship, either right before or right after; the Antichrist comes on the scene.

Israel is a ticking clock that is at five minutes to midnight!

Look up fellow Christian, our redemption is nigh. Jesus is coming soon. We fit the description of that last and final generation upon the earth when Messiah comes for us. The spiritual and moral conditions are apparent. The one-world financial and judicial system is in place. The political beast is roaring. The Church of the Laodiceans is here. The whole world "groaneth in travail" awaiting the redemption that is to come.

The 6,000th year is ticking down; the final Jubilee is on the horizon. Israel is seeking peace while the Church is seeking pleasure. The whole world is a powder keg waiting to explode.
A harvest is coming.
The Antichrist is coming.
Everything is about to change.

Seven clocks
all ticking
towards the
same
end-time
event

Time Is Running Out!

Everything is about to change. The trumpet in Heaven will sound, the Church will be caught away. Once the saints are gone, it will be TOO LATE for those who are not saved. Friend, the time is short: we are truly at the end of all things! The world will begin to experience God's almighty and impending wrath.

Look what the Bible says about this terrible time:

Matthew 24:21 *"For then shall be great tribulation, such as was not since the beginning of the world to this time, no, nor ever shall be."*

Friend, look at just some of the horror that will be poured out upon the earth during the Tribulation:

Revelation 6:8 *"And I looked, and behold a pale horse: and his name that sat on him was Death, and Hell followed with him. And power was given unto them over the fourth part of the earth, to kill with sword, and with hunger, and with death, and with the beasts of the earth."*

Revelation 6:16-17 *"[16]And said to the mountains and rocks, Fall on us, and hide us from the face of him thatsitteth on the throne, and from the wrath of the Lamb: [17]For the great day of his wrath is come; and who shall be able to stand?"*

Revelation 9:1-2 *"[1]And the fifth angel sounded, and I saw a star fall from heaven unto the earth: and to him was given the key of the bottomless pit. [2]And he opened the bottomless pit; and there arose a smoke out of the pit, as the smoke of a great furnace; and the sun and the air were darkened by reason of the smoke of the pit."*

Revelation 9:5-6 *"[5]And to them it was given that they should not kill them, but that they should be tormented five months: and their torment was as the torment of a scorpion, when he striketh a man. [6]And in those days shall men seek death, and shall not find it; and shall desire to die, and death shall flee from them."*

Can you imagine a world without Christians? Imagine that all the Bible-believing churches are empty. Worse yet, imagine living in a world *without* God for seven years. The Tribulation is a time of wrath from God upon Satan, and upon those who reject the Lord Jesus Christ; the stage is set for all these events to begin.

The hour is later than you think. Friend, are you prepared to meet the Lord? Are you ready for the trumpet to sound? Are you "rapture ready?"

What you need to be "rapture ready".

You must be a saved born-again child of God.
To be saved you first need to see yourself as God sees you, a

sinner under the condemnation of a holy God.

Romans 3:10 *"As it is written, There is none righteous, no, not one."*

Romans 3:23 *"For all have sinned, and come short of the glory of God;"*

Romans 6:23 *"For the wages of sin is death; but the gift of God is eternal life through Jesus Christ our Lord."*

The sinner faces death and Hell as his payment for sin. God's gift is salvation when we trust in the Lord Jesus Christ and His blood that was shed for our sin on the cross of Calvary

Romans 6:23 *"For the wages of sin is death; but the gift of God is eternal life through Jesus Christ our Lord."*

Romans 10:9-13 *"**9**That if thou shalt confess with thy mouth the Lord Jesus, and shalt believe in thine heart that God hath raised him from the dead, thou shalt be saved. **10**For with the heart man believeth unto righteousness; and with the mouth confession is made unto salvation. **11**For the scripture saith, Whosoever believeth on him shall not be ashamed. **12**For there is no difference between the Jew and the Greek: for the same Lord over all is rich unto all that call upon him. **13**For whosoever shall call upon the name of the Lord shall be saved."*

The time is now. Friend, simply bow your head and admit to God that you are a sinner on your way to an eternity in Hell. Repent of your unbelief and place your trust in the Lord Jesus Christ to wash away your sins and save you from the penalty of your sin. Put your complete faith and trust in Christ and be saved, believing that Jesus is the virgin born Son of God who died, was buried, and rose from the grave to pay your sin debt.

John 3:16 "For God so loved the world, that he gave his only begotten Son, that whosoever believeth in him should not perish, but have everlasting life."

If you have prayed this prayer from your heart, Friend, you are saved and ready to be "caught up" to meet the Saviour, Jesus Christ.

Romans 10:13 *"For whosoever shall call upon the name of the Lord* ***shall*** *be saved."*

Congratulations! You are now saved from the wrath to come and will spend eternity in heaven!

Other helps to guide you to be rapture ready:

1. As you await His return, allow yourself to be guided by the Bible to *live a life pleasing to God.*

1Peter 1:16 *"Because it is written, Be ye holy; for I am holy."*

Read, read, read the Word of God! He infuses it with His Spirit, and it will bring you peace.

2. Watch for the Lord's return. That means to be aware of the signs happening in the world around you in relation to the Biblical prophecies, especially as discussed in previous chapters.

Matthew 24:42 *"Watch therefore: for ye know not what hour your Lord doth come."*

Look at the special blessing for those who watch:

Luke 12:37 *"Blessed are those servants, whom the lord when he cometh shall find watching: verily I say unto you, that he shall gird himself, and make them to sit down to meat, and will come forth and serve them."*

Does this mean that in heaven, Jesus will serve the 'watchers' when they sit down to eat? What a thought! What a blessing!

I hope and pray that you are saved and are watching for the Lord's return. It will be very soon.

Print by Neal Holland

MORE FROM GOODWIN PUBLICATIONS
at
www.godsfinaljubilee.com

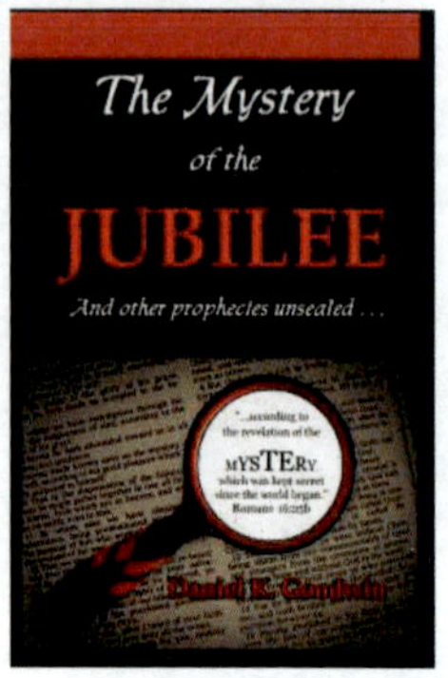

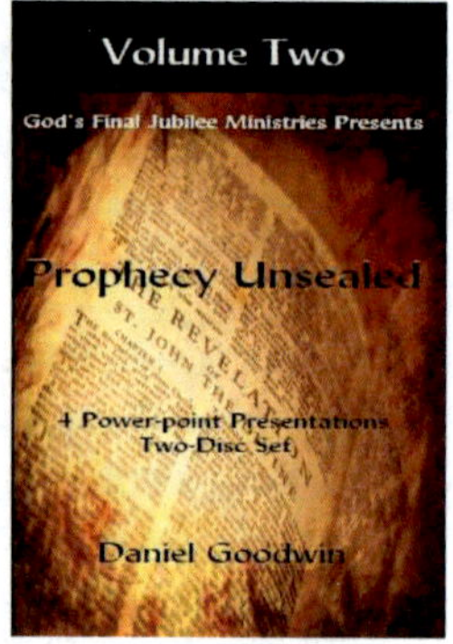

Volume 1 & 2 DVD Sets

Dan Goodwin
117 E. 18th St #165
Owensboro, KY 42303

814-599-6280 (Text or call)

daniel@godsfinaljubilee.com